W9-BMY-437

THE ANCIENT SYMBOLIC LANDSCAPE OF WESSEX

David Ride

AMBERLEY

*I dedicate this book to my supremely supportive wife Sandra,
and to the overthrowing of irrational disbelief*

First published 2010

Amberley Publishing
Cirencester Road, Chalford,
Stroud, Gloucestershire GL6 8PE

www.amberleybooks.com

Copyright © David Ride, 2010

The right of David Ride to be identified as the Author
of this work has been asserted in accordance with the
Copyrights, Designs and Patents Act 1988.

All rights reserved. No part of this book may be reprinted
or reproduced or utilised in any form or by any electronic,
mechanical or other means, now known or hereafter invented, including
photocopying and recording, or in any information
storage or retrieval system, without the permission in writing
from the Publishers.

British Library Cataloguing in Publication Data.
A catalogue record for this book is available from the British Library.

ISBN 978-1-4456-0169-4

Typesetting and Origination by Amberley Publishing.
Printed in Great Britain.

CONTENTS

NOTE TO THE READER

Readers are assured that the terrestrial distances and directions given in this book have been calculated by a specially written computer program named **ALFREDA**, which stands for **A L**ine **F**itting **R**outine and **E**valuator of **D**istances and **A**zimuths. Sites are entered into the routine using their co-ordinates, to the nearest metre, either as National Grid References or as latitude and longitude, and can be stored in a library on disc for retrieval as necessary. If sites are more or less linearly arranged, the best fit of a great circle through them is calculated, together with individual divergences from the line. Distances between sites and the directions (azimuths) formed by pairs of sites can be computed. The curvature of the earth is considered in these calculations, and the routine can operate to an accuracy of one metre of distance and one-hundredth part of a degree of arc.

ACKNOWLEDGEMENTS

I am grateful to the following people for their generous help: Reverend Jacquie Birdseye, Rector of Moreton Church, for permission to include my images of the church and a window by Laurence Whistler; Andrew Easton for permission to reproduce his fine view of sunrise over Lowestoft Ness; Graham Cooper of www.newforest.hampshire.org.uk for allowing me to download the image from the Drivers' map of the New Forest; the churchwardens of Waltham Abbey for agreeing to let me reproduce my image of the statue of King Harold; Iain Scott, Assistant Director of the legal department of Glasgow City Council, for advice on reproducing the former Arms of the City of Glasgow; the Librarian of the Folklore Society for permission to quote from the Reverend J. H. Weeks; the Hampshire County Council Archaeological Service for information from their Archaeological and Historic Building Record; the Administrator of the Royal Archaeological Institute, for approving my sketch of the Dorset Cursus, based on the paper by A. Penny and J. E. Wood in *The Archaeological Journal*; Kathryn Charles-Wilson of the British Museum for helpful advice on reproducing my image of the *djed*; Michael Harvey for sorting out my computer at vital moments; the Reverend Professor P. Curzen and Professor R. F. Griffiths for their enthusiastic encouragement; Duncan Shortland for helpful comments on the text as it evolved; Louise Ford for proof-reading assistance; Alan Sutton of Amberley Publishing for accepting my manuscript for publication; and Robert Drew, my Project Editor, for many helpful and patient suggestions for its improvement.

A VISION OF ENGLAND

To the serious user or the mere browser, maps are magical. The archetypal map is a picture of the ground, a collection of dots on flat parchment, each representing a city, town or village, with black lines masquerading as roads linking them, with sinuous blue lines denoting rivers separating them, with green, shrouding blocks mimicking the forests surrounding them. An area of an oceanic hue will abut solid ground, populated only by a few scudding ships and exotic creatures of the sea. All the mapmaker has to do is to establish where everything lies in relation to everything else; to decide what to leave out; to scribe in conventional symbols on parchment or copper plate what is most important; and add a few flourishes.

Gerard Mercator was a master mapmaker, but why did he write despairingly, in a letter to the French philosopher Jean Bodin: 'I am amazed that a learned man makes judgements so glibly about matters either not understood or not clearly examined'? This is a cry that resonates from my own heart, for some of the most able minds in academia have misrepresented and rejected the pages that follow. By any measure of logic or statistics, what I have discovered cannot be an artefact of chance, yet giants of intellect will have it so.

The magic of maps resides in their property to display a county, country, continent or the cosmos on one intelligible page. We can roam at will over land, sea or sky, lingering in some region of fascination or shooting on some whim, faster than the speed of light, to a remoter spot. By purchasing an atlas we become citizens of the universe, tourists of the known regions, pundits of geography.

But what of Mercator's despair? There is a single-word answer: politics. Maps are not just delightful works of art or useful tools for finding your way home. Maps are the most intensely political documents yet contrived. For a start, maps define boundaries: this is *my* land. Are the names written in French or German, in Russian or Chinese, in Welsh or English? Language is a potent denominator of ownership and control. And what about those scrolled and beribboned cartouches, the ones that tell the reader who commissioned the map, paid for it, and published it to the world? Therein lies the affirmation of *power*. Maps are the indispensable instruments of those who need to supervise or yearn to tyrannise.

But not all maps are paper or parchment simulacra of portions of the universe. One fine evening when I stood just inland in Norfolk, a perfect image of the land appeared in the sky. A sheet of cloud mapped part of East Anglia, perhaps more than my limited horizon revealed. Every part of the aerial coastline matched the zenith of its sandy counterpart; every mote of the sheet formed an analogue of the acre beneath it. There, aloft, stood the Wash's fenny calyx: there, Norfolk's lordotic hunch.

Observers of yore would have seen a miraculous celestial map, but the prosaic explanation for the phenomenon is straightforward. The land and sea surfaces were at different temperatures, and so radiated heat back to space at different wavelengths. Aloft, at some 14,000 feet, was a layer of humid air. Water vapour is readily transparent to some wavelengths of heat – that which was radiated by the sea that evening, obviously – but less so to that which was emitted from the land then. The lower levels of the mixture of water vapour and air high over the land absorbed this heat energy; they warmed up and set off a honeycomb of convection cells, like the bubbles in boiling marmalade. As the humid air rose in each cell, it expanded owing to the decrease in atmospheric pressure that occurs with increased height. The energy for this expansion came from the mixture itself, and it cooled down to a point where the air became saturated; a myriad of tiny clouds formed a pellucid stratum.

However, in the milky pointillism of the nascent altocumulus lay its own destruction: the clouds cut off the rays of the sun and the surface temperature dropped; the critical balance of energy necessary to sustain convection was upset. Yet before East Anglia reverted totally from opaque droplets to invisible vapour and dissolved into a blue, celestial North Sea, the sun's increasingly low angle illuminated the cloud sheet from below, infusing the fading map with the rich, spectacular blush of sunset. Like the rest of the British Empire, Norfolk was painted red, then disappeared.

I related this experience to my meteorological friends (I moved in such circles then). 'Most improbable!' was the reaction. But I *saw* it. 'Hmmph!' Oh, Mercator, Mercator!

I had seen the earth mapped on the sky. Why, then, should the sky not be mapped on the earth? What would be the politics of that exercise? Instead of an antique and precious sheet of parchment depicting wide dominions, emblazoned with escutcheons of authority and cartouches proclaiming sovereign mandates from God, here would be the real thing, the landscape itself, not spattered with cartoons of power but with power's instruments themselves – cities, cathedrals, churches, castles, ports, prisons and palaces – overlain with the cartographic elements of celestial constellations and co-ordinates. How powerfully political: how politically powerful. How magical!

David Ride
Salisbury, 2010

1

THE IMPOSITION OF SPATIAL ORDER ON THE LANDSCAPE

Unless we allow for [the] innate capacity of the human mind to entertain contradictory beliefs at the same time, we shall in vain attempt to understand the history of thought in general and of religion in particular.

Reverend John H. Weeks (*Folk-lore*, XX)

My Big Bang

Cosmologists tell us that our universe began about 14 billion years ago as a tiny speck of intensely hot and dense elementary particles that gradually cooled, consolidated into matter, and expanded to the dimensions observed today. This book derives from a similar process but has only taken three and a half decades.

For many years, I entertained an interest in the legends surrounding the killing of William II – Rufus – in Canterton Glen in the New Forest. I focused in on the Rufus Stone, where legend alone tells he fell, unaware of that site's true significance. Suddenly, my intense concentration on that enigmatic monument reached bursting point, and I discovered myself gazing at a rapidly expanding 'universe' of landscape inhabited by stars and other features of the sky. My personal Big Bang had arrived.

My interest in the ritual sites of southern England coincided with the rise of landscape archaeology, the study of signs left by mankind's interaction with his local terrain, and extended through 1965, when proof of the cosmological Big Bang was provided by the undisputed reception of the microwave radiation left over from the initial expansion radiating back from the edges of the universe.

The current Rufus Stone in Canterton Glen in the New Forest.

Ritual landscapes

Notable examples of ritual landscapes in Britain include Stonehenge and its environs, its barrows and cursūs clustered in expanding ripples about the earthen and stone circles of the central monument, and the associated earthwork of Durrington Walls. The Avebury complex is also a truly monumental ritual landscape, containing a chambered long barrow, processional avenues and an artificial mountain, Silbury Hill, in addition to its huge circles of earth and stone. Outside Britain, the temple complexes at Karnac in Egypt and Palenque in Mexico constitute examples of ritual landscapes.

Landscape archaeology is not quite *de rigueur* for some archaeologists. The discipline becomes lonelier when one leaves the social and economic factors determining land use and instead studies ritual sites – those deemed (not always justifiably) to be wholly or mostly concerned with the enactment of rituals associated with the 'other world'. The excavation of elements within such landscapes remains 'mainstream', for it involves the gathering of evidence. Controversy begins when the evidence is interpreted. As I write, two new evidence-based theories of Stonehenge have been posited. The first claims that 'the whole purpose of Stonehenge is that it was a prehistoric Lourdes', based on the discovery of a disproportionate number of diseased skeletons there and assemblages of bluestone chippings. The second states that Stonehenge is the repository of the ashes and bones of the elect, brought there from Durrington Walls, which was the scene of mass Neolithic wakes. The interpretation in this case rests in part on the discovery of huge numbers of cooked pig bones on site. One would like to divide theories into those that are merely consistent with the evidence and those that are demanded by it. However, the generally fragmentary nature of archaeological evidence precludes such an indulgence. Usually, the most we can do is concoct an index of merit based on the evidence offered and the quality of the arguments, and stand ready to change our views when fresh evidence emerges or superior arguments are presented. I hope that my theories will be judged in this way too, and not on the basis of some initial prejudice.

Stonehenge and such sites, whatever the interpretations of them may be, are public statements of ritual endeavour and contemporary public recognition, for much of the population would have been employed in their construction. There, the erection of ritual monuments and the performance of ritual procedures within them were obviously overt societal practices, incapable of concealment, if not of full comprehension and participation.

Symbolic landscapes

Let's move on to even lonelier territory, the study of what I prefer to call 'symbolic landscapes', a term better fitted to their philosophical basis than the often-used 'sacred landscape', where only mystery, not sacredness, can be inferred to exist. These may be more extensive than ritual landscapes but will almost certainly contain ritual sites. They need to possess man-made or convenient natural features to define them.

That rituals, symbols and myths became intimately associated with special locations can be merely part of the process whereby landscape forms the repository of personal and collective memories: *here* we always watch for midsummer's sunrise; *here* are kept the bones of our ancestors; *there* is where we feast with our neighbours. Hallowed ground is often formed by haphazard habit. This is one method by which terrain operates on human consciousness, but intentional, intellectual processes are at work too. Symbolic landscapes are patterned landscapes, even if not by construction then by designation. Powerful as are the religious motivations to construct them, there exist sound practical reasons based in the politics of control. For instance, the possession of technical knowledge, or merely the gift of remembering recurring sequences, imparts the ability to predict the future; such prophetic arts confer the power to control. On the one hand stand the captains and the intellectuals capable of moulding features of the earth into co-ordinated, impressive symbols, and on the other the hordes that wait to be impressed.

In his *Landscape and memory*, Simon Schama, the art historian, contends that the cults of the primitive forest, the river of life, and the sacred mountain are present in the landscape if only we know where to look for them. That is one purpose of this book: to seek them out. We shall discover what lies at the heart of the primitive forest, identify the river of life and the primeval mound, but not without clues to focus our vision.

The recognisable patterns within symbolic landscapes are formed from buildings, monuments, or surveyed 'sketches' of ritually endowed objects, combined according to a set of thematic rules. Fortuitously occurring natural features can be worked into the scheme. Vincent Scully (*The earth, the temple, and the gods: Greek sacred architecture*) has confirmed just how ancient and widespread was mankind's perception of a symbolic landscape, and how man-made features can be amalgamated with natural ones to give specific meaning to an area. He studied over 150 temples scattered across Greece, finding the presence of repeating landscape elements that together are clearly representative of human forms, their sexual characteristics depending on the gender of the deity inhabiting a temple. Scully discovered recurring patterns in these symbolic landscapes. These are not overt structures; they need searching for by someone who has obtained a clue to their existence, or maybe has stumbled on one by chance, perhaps with the curiosity to enquire if an initially spotted suggestive pattern is repeated elsewhere. Until discovered by Scully, they were not generally recognised, suggesting that knowledge of them had been lost, or was restricted.

The American social geographer Donald W. Meinig (*Symbolic landscapes*) postulates that all mature nations possess their own unique symbolic landscape featuring their shared experiences and philosophy, a system that provides them with a national identity. So where are all these other landscapes? The historian and broadcaster Michael Wood (*In search of England*) may have an answer to this question. He writes that the British once possessed an ancient religious language of symbols and words, but the belief system that supported it disappeared, rendering it meaningless to its heirs. If this is so, our efforts to recover the symbolic landscape will be aided by seeking an understanding of the belief system once in operation, as well as cultural practices.

An important feature of a symbolic landscape is that mundane, secular activities can occur within it; the symbol can be so large that it spans a whole territory containing other social and economic activities – too large to see unless searched for piecewise, perhaps. The moot question is, of course: what does a symbolic landscape symbolise?

A line of inquiry

Arguably, the simplest patterned symbolic landscape consists of an axis. Solstitial axes are generally accepted as deliberate alignments at Stonehenge, Newgrange and Abu Simbel. A more modern example is the Great Axis of Paris, begun in 1616 when Marie de' Medici created the park known as the Champs-Élysées. In 1640, Le Nôtre, who designed the gardens at Versailles, planted there a row of elm trees leading away from the Louvre, originally the palace of the kings of France. The most magnificent room in the Louvre is the Apollo Gallery, dating from the reign of Louis XIV. From there, the Axis passes through the Arc de Triomphe du Carrousel; the Egyptian obelisk of Rameses II, one of a pair taken from Luxor and representing the setting sun; the Arc de Triomphe de l'Étoile; and now, the Grande Arche at the Tête Défence, opened on 14 July 1989. The Great Axis is being continually extended as chance permits. It is essentially a line concerned with the afterlife, for it is the median line of the Champs-Élysées, the Elysian Fields, which were the abode of good souls after death. The visitors' entrance to the Louvre is through an incongruous, modern glass pyramid that lies on the Paris Meridian. One descends from the pyramid into the underworld where, after paying the ferryman at the till, one is permitted to ascend the Stygian escalator to the wonders above.

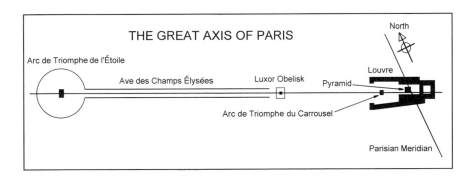

Grand country houses in England and elsewhere were often furnished with an axis, a line at right angles to the frontage of the house, terminating in an obelisk or other prominent feature. The example of the Parisian Axis suggests that such lines were not simply fashionable architectural features but carried a symbolic meaning. William Benson, who supplanted Sir Christopher Wren as Surveyor General of the King's Works, built Wilbury, a Palladian villa in south Wiltshire in 1711, siting it so that its axis was at right angles to the line from the front door to the summit of a distant hill, on the crest of which he erected a medieval gatehouse that had formerly stood at Amesbury Abbey. The distance from the central cupola of the house to the gatehouse was exactly two miles, the supposition being that he intended to use the line as the baseline for the cartographical survey of England. In practice it was far too short; the survey was eventually based on a line reaching from Old Sarum to Beacon Hill near Amesbury in 1794. Benson's gatehouse fell down, but the Ordnance Survey used a little plinth of bricks on the remaining mound as a tertiary trigonometrical point. Benson was a strange man, a control freak addicted to weird esoteric rituals; he eventually went mad. Perhaps he had been aware that his gatehouse stood on the longest east–west line in England (a line of latitude), stretching from coast to coast, from St Margaret's at Cliffe in the east to Baggy Point in the west.

Axes are necessarily directional, thus encoding another piece of potentially useful information. In *Prehistoric astronomy and ritual*, Aubrey Burl, an authority on prehistoric stone circles, points to a general recognition among modern archaeologists that orientation ranks alongside artefacts and architecture as clues to understanding ritual sites. This is a clear and authoritative endorsement of a spatial characteristic once often neglected. There are at least two ways that directional data can be considered: one is in relation to features of the wider landscape, perhaps an alignment to a prominent natural feature, as with Benson's axis; the other is as an indicator of membership of a general class of sites, when, say, the doorways of Iron Age round houses favour an orientation to the south-east. In the second case, the concept of a model is employed, which may be used to obtain insights of an inferential nature using information from similar sites, and to establish or confirm general properties of the model and its limits of application. Such thinking will be useful to our inquiry.

We leave this discussion enriched by the knowledge that such simple features as axes can be endowed with meaningful complexity; that they have ancient antecedents; that they are favoured by rich and powerful men; and that they may be the result of accurate surveys. What is needed now is a philosophy for their construction and the developmental process leading to it.

How it all started

Mathematics probably began with arithmetic, with the need for counting. How many men were there in the tribe; how many breeding women; how many mouths to feed? Next came measurement, first in terms of counting: how many days' journey away is the hunting ground? Then came measurement in terms of a unit of length: how many strides' width is the river? Here lies a deep philosophical point: distance for a walking man can, for practical purposes, be measured both in units of *time* and of *length*. But it would be millennia before this point became an issue for realisation, resolution and harmonisation, processes that I shall examine in this work. Arithmetic was thus grounded in practical needs. Geometry came next, the term meaning 'measurement of the earth'. It involved, before it was idealised by the Greeks, both arithmetic and the concept of shape. Natural shapes were hardly ever regular: certainly, one could stare indefinitely at the circle of the full moon, but most things – coastlines and rivers, for example – possessed irregular shapes, needful of investigation and demanding description. From long ago, the stride or the dimensions of parts of the human body were used for measurements when required. Man-made shapes could exist as circular or rectangular buildings, triangular corrals or polygonal field boundaries. Consideration of the relative positions of three cities, say, was a matter of shape but it also produced the concept of the map.

Then there were the shapes in the night sky. The human brain, unconsciously eager to group stars together to produce a familiar form, could recognise the imperative clusterings of the constellations of Cassiopeia, Ursa Major, the Square of Pegasus, and the compellingly anthropomorphic figure of Orion. The human tongue gave them names, unlikely at first to be the ones employed here. The concept of 'name it, know it' began to impart familiarity to these constellations, casting them as subjects of imaginative stories, creating myths. The brilliant beauty of the night sky could not be ignored, and it was noticed that these constellations wheeled nightly about a point in the heavens, each one rising above the horizon at the same point – as seen from a fixed location – but at different times throughout the seasons (unless it was a constellation that never set, like the Plough as seen from Britain). In these majestic circular motions and seasonal differences was the science of astronomy born. The disposition of the sun and stars could be used as an annual clock to regulate the sowing and harvesting of crops and the celebration of festivals. But what of the moon? In general, it stood higher in the sky in summer than in winter, but it possessed cycles and phases of peculiar duration, regular but maddeningly complex compared with the sun, which roamed the earth daily and the heavens annually. And what of the planets, those 'wandering stars', some of which appeared to perform loops among the pattern formed by those stars that maintained constant positions with respect to one another? As trades and professions became specialised with the advent of civil and political advances in civilisation, there was much for the new professional astronomers to study and speculate about.

Some elementary cosmology

To study the movement of the stars, one needs a framework within which to position them, one that necessarily moves together with the stars relative to an observer; alternatively, one needs a fixed background against which to measure their motions. The astronomers were faced with a simple choice. They chose to give the sky its own framework in which the stars were set and to consider the motion of the stars and the framework together relative to the horizon of the earth or to some structure, natural or otherwise, which could serve as a terrestrial reference or datum – an observatory. Professor Alexander Thom (*Megalithic sites in Britain* and *Megalithic lunar observatories*) catalogued many natural observatories used in Neolithic times for the sun and moon. Professor John North described other prehistoric structures for observing stars (*Stonehenge: Neolithic man and the cosmos*).

For all the practical purposes of the time, the star pattern could be considered as unchanging and stuck to the inside of a vast sphere whose centre coincided with the centre of the earth. The sphere apparently turned constantly about an axis; although, in reality, it was the earth that turned in a contrary direction about this axis; and as the earth's axis passes through the two terrestrial poles, the axis of the celestial sphere, a continuation of the earth's axis through space, passes through the celestial poles. It is generally believed that astronomy developed first in the northern hemisphere, and people dwelling north of the terrestrial equator could see the stars rotating about the north celestial pole. Other celestial references were needed. The celestial sphere had its own equator and circles of 'latitude' equivalent to the circles of latitude on earth, except that we refer to them now as 'declinations'. Meridians, equivalent to lines of terrestrial longitude, were constructed, now named (in astronomers' jargon) 'right ascensions'. In short, the celestial sphere was gridded up, just as the earth is gridded up for reference purposes, with its own equivalents of latitudes and longitudes.

This process took time to develop, with the celestial pole as the first probable fixed point of reference, but it is clear from the process of development that a correspondence was recognised between the firmament and the surface of the earth. The awesome beauty of the revolving night sky and the anthropomorphic associations of some constellations consolidated religious philosophy into a scheme in which huge and splendid celestial creatures influenced, if not dominated, the lives of their paler and far less significant images on earth. Above cycled permanent gods; below toiled transient men. Supreme was the sun, unrivalled in the essential light and heat it conferred on the earth. It is easy to appreciate the concept of 'as above, so below' that came to characterise astronomically-based religious thought. How better to perfect an imperfect earth than by reproducing the geography of a perfect heaven on the surface of our globe? He who could perform this feat would generate and wield great power. The concept of the astronomer priest was born, a person of knowledge and wisdom who understood the motions of the heavens, who could predict the disposition of the stars and the times of eclipses. Such a person, in touch with heaven, could legitimise a man in the position of king, and in return receive protection and resources from him. It is a reciprocal situation that persists in Britain today, although the job specification for the Archbishop of Canterbury no longer requires a doctoral degree in astronomy.

Religion requires its temples, for rituals of praise, sacrifice, propitiation, and supplication – all conducted as much to control the ordinary citizen with dramas of awe and fear as to placate and entreat the gods with rituals productive of blood, smoke, noise, and motion. The greater the prestige associated with a temple, and hence its priests and their acolytes, the greater the power exerted by them. No doubt national rivalries existed between temples vying for international congregations or pilgrims. What, then, could confer legitimacy and prestige upon a temple? Tradition was one element: rites were conducted at sites where rites had been conducted for longer than tribal memories existed. Sanctification was another: a temple site was one where miracles had happened or a holy man had dwelt. But these are subjective and historical reasons; what conferred legitimacy most of all was the objective property of demonstrably mirroring a significant point of the firmament. Such a correspondence directly connected earth with heaven, the ephemeral consciousness of 'the here' with the permanent and serene existence of 'the above'.

19

What bothers mortals most is their mortality. Escape to the endless bliss of the skies is a preoccupation worthy of pursuit and the expenditure of great resources. In some cultures, it was sufficient to expedite the passage of the ephemeral essence of an individual, 'the soul'; in others, such as that of the ancient Egyptians, it was necessary to ensure the departed spirit's eventual rehabilitation of its earthly body by its preservation through mummification. Yet other philosophies postulated a halfway position, with an extant soul returning to occupy a fresh body through the process of reincarnation. No matter the fine detail, all processes of achieving life after death devolved upon establishing a 'legitimate' temple or sepulchre, often the same structure, whose authority and legitimacy could be demonstrated clearly as an earth–heaven conduit. Salvation has been sought by individuals independently of priest or mausoleum only lately.

How could this astronomical legitimacy of temples be achieved? It is not sufficient simply to designate a temple as the analogue of, say, the star Betelgeuse. There has to be some way of demonstrating that the 'dedication' is unequivocally to Betelgeuse and not to Capella, or any other star. One way would be to survey and erect a pattern of temples over an area of countryside that exactly mirrored the shape of the constellation of Orion, of which Betelgeuse is a component star. Unless the temples were unreasonably close to one another, one characteristic of such a constellation map would be that it is too large to be seen from the ground, but such a property can be viewed as an advantage. In some cultures, this kind of knowledge is regarded as privileged, to be imparted to a neophyte only after a period of instruction, examination, and ordination or initiation. Such a process creates or enforces exclusivity, and thereby concentrates power. Neophytes are screened for 'suitability', that is, orthodoxy of personal philosophy and conduct, and the attainment of knowledge is dependent upon a promise of secrecy, loyalty, and conformity to the group's interests. It follows from this situation that documentary evidence for any pattern of stars or astronomical structures in the landscape is likely to be elusive. Fortunately, the landscape itself cannot be concealed, although teasing out its secrets may be laborious.

Another way to ensure legitimacy is to survey and mark on the ground in some way the framework imposed on the heavens, instead of the constellations themselves. Once again, it is insufficient to designate a temple as the celestial north pole without also marking at least some images of those lines and nodes of the celestial framework that pass through the pole or bear a recognisable relationship to it. The lines and points of interest in antiquity are well known;

they are the ones apparent on armillary spheres. Only those in the northern hemisphere will concern us; they are the celestial pole, the tropic of Cancer (that is, the circle of declination through the position occupied by the sun at the summer solstice, about 23½ degrees north), the celestial equator, the circle of the ecliptic (the plane of which lies at about 23½ degrees to the equatorial plane and cuts it at the vernal equinox), and two circles of right ascension, the one passing through the vernal equinox and the other at ninety degrees to it (known as the solstitial colure and passing through the solstitial point of the sun on the ecliptic). Another point of interest is the ecliptic pole that lies about 23½ degrees from the celestial pole and resides on the solstitial colure. Some of these terms may be unfamiliar to the reader; they will be explained in detail when we encounter them again, and a glossary has also been supplied at the back of the book.

I have used the phrase 'about 23½ degrees' for the tilt of the ecliptic and positions whose angles mirror and depend on this tilt; the precise value changes slightly over millennia, and discovery of the value used in the surveyed pattern indicates, within limits determined by the accuracy of observation and replication, at what date the survey was made.

There is one further way that the earth's surface can be used as an astronomical sketchpad, and that is to reproduce on it the mythology assigned to the stars. This may be performed by mixing together the constellations and armillary lines in combinations not observed in the heavens, and including among them shapes that possess no heavenly analogues but add to the meaning of the patterns thus formed – the so-called *capriccio* view used by artists for centuries to condense a landscape canvas and manufacture a pleasing composition.

Cues to spatial order

Do such patterns exist; are there 'hidden' symbolic landscapes? The Pythagoreans, for example, pledged to kill those of their members who revealed secrets of the brotherhood. They were followers of Pythagoras of Samos, the sixth-century BC Ionian philosopher and mathematician whose influence on Plato caused Greek ideas to permeate all western philosophy. One sect of them interwove their esoteric and mystical beliefs with mathematics. The eminent British philosopher and mathematician Bertrand Russell admits in his *Autobiography* that he yearned to know why the stars shine, and to capture an understanding of the power exerted by Pythagorean numerical philosophy. Russell was echoing a widespread feeling.

It is a valid question to ask if such societies constructed their own covert symbolic landscapes. If so, they would not be conspicuous. Professor Wendy Ashmore and Dr A. Bernard Knapp (*Archaeologies of landscape*) comment that meaning in a landscape is not directly related to how distinctively it has been marked in archaeologically detectable ways. Ashmore and Knapp also suggest that 'Perhaps more often than has been recognised, the sky provides the cues to spatial order on the terrestrial plane', citing authors with similar views in support. Their statements convey the possibility that the earth may have been tattooed to mirror the sky but proving it could be difficult. How, then, shall we search for 'Pythagorean' landscape structures? What are their characteristics? Even with the tentative encouragement of Ashmore and Knapp, the situation is not straightforward, for the skies display not only the static spectacles of prominent stars and notable constellations, but also the points and circles established by the dynamics of the heavens and mankind's efforts to formalise them.

The topic has not got off to a propitious start. John Michell (*New light on the ancient mysteries of Glastonbury*) suggested that seven hills around Glastonbury – which were once islands – were anciently considered to represent the constellation of the Plough, but the match of patterns is very poor and there is no additional supporting evidence for the notion. Earlier, in 1929, Kathleen Maltwood (*A guide to Glastonbury's temple of the stars*) proposed an intentionally surveyed Glastonbury Zodiac, but again the correspondences between icons of the zodiacal constellations and terrestrial features were poor at best, and mostly patently fanciful. Others have constructed similar fanciful patterns, but none has had the strength to surface into the academic world. If a Pythagorean pattern exists, its principal characteristic must be accuracy, one consistent with the brotherhood's concern for precision, and with a contemporary observer's skill to measure angles in the sky and reproduce them on the ground.

Not a wholly bad book

The book *Hamlet's mill* by Georgio de Santillana and Hertha von Dechend, both professors in the field of the history of science, deals with ancient mythology. It aims to appeal to a general readership, but has received much academic criticism. Its stated aim of proving that all mythology derives from the heavens is vulnerable to the production of one myth that is clearly not of celestial origin. However, the authors have performed a great service by

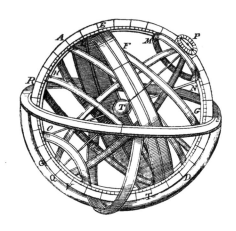

An armillary sphere, from *Chambers'*
Cyclopaedia, c. 1760.

documenting and illustrating a little-known concept of an almost worldwide
notion of a cosmic axis, also described as the World Tree or Tree of Life, or the
axis mundi, which exists as some form of terrestrial analogue with its origin
located in a maritime whirlpool, from which the energy of symbolic celestial
rotation can be imagined to derive, and which axis they associate with the
solstitial colure (a celestial meridian that runs through the sky at the point
where the sun lies at a solstitial position, that is, the highest or lowest point
it achieves in the sky). De Santillana and von Dechend maintained that the
concept also included other circles of the armillary sphere.

As the Tree of Life, there are many examples of the cosmic axis. In
Scandinavian myth it is Yggdrasil, the ash tree, created by Allfather. It took
root in the underworld, and its branches overshadowed Odin's Hall and
other worlds. On it, Odin hung for nine days and nights, thereby winning the
knowledge of runes, which gave him power over all the earth. (Odin became
Woden among the Saxons.) The origin of this myth lies in ancient Greece,
where the sacred king was dedicated to the ash tree (see Robert Graves, *The
Greek myths*). Three Norns stood at the base of Yggdrasil, dispensing justice.
The parallel with Christ's cross, around which gathered the three Marys, is
striking; few Christians would dispute that the cross is a suitable symbol for
the Tree of Life, but it has ancient antecedents. One of these is the biblical
Jacob's Ladder, which stretched from the stone he erected at Bethel ('House of
God'), and on which he dreamed that angels descended from heaven and rose
again. The stone of Bethel is clearly a conduit point, such as we have discussed.
An important point arises here: Jacob's Ladders, once favoured by jobbing
builders but now banned from use by the Health and Safety Executive, consist

of a central pole with rungs fixed to it at equal intervals. In a very obvious manner, the pole is graduated: it forms a linear scale. However, the origin of the Tree of Life probably lies with the *djed* pillar in ancient Egypt, but the *djed* requires a chapter of its own.

What are we looking for?

Let's list the features that a Pythagorean landscape might contain. There are the cosmological ones: a significantly orientated cosmic axis and associated celestial circles; images of constellations, together with analogues of particularly prominent stars and positions like the solstitial and equinoctial points; and the celestial and ecliptic poles. The fundamental philosophy of the Pythagoreans was based on number. They ascribed particular characteristics to the first few positive integers; thus six was the number of perfection, the first 'perfect number', the sum of its divisors excluding itself (6 = 1 + 2 + 3). We might therefore expect to find line segments consisting of a whole number of a common unit of length.

Non-integers were dealt with by means of proportions, characterised by the ratios of the lengths of line segments. For example, three of the numbers of interest to the Pythagoreans were pi (π), (approximately 3.14159), the square root of two (approximately 1.41421), and the Golden Mean (approximately 1.61803 – or its reciprocal, 0.61803). None of these numbers can be precisely expressed as the ratio of two integers, but their approximations have practical use. Approximations to the Golden Mean can be derived from the anciently known Fibonacci series where every succeeding term is the sum of the two that preceded it. (Some purists demand that the first two numbers should always be 0 and 1, but this is unnecessarily restrictive.) After some initial oscillation, the ratio of two adjacent terms tends more closely to the Golden Mean as the series progresses. Thus 9, 40, 49, 89, 138, 227, 365, 592, 957, 1549, 2506, 4055, 6561 are the first thirteen terms of such a series providing a final good estimate for the Golden Mean of 1.618002 (6561/4055). This particular segment of the series has as its central value the number of days in a year and is capable of bearing much symbolic meaning. Also note that 6561 results from the number three raised to the power of eight ($3 \times 3 = 9$; $9 \times 9 = 81$; $81 \times 81 = 6561$). These results are presented here to demonstrate the symbolic potential of numerology and for use later.

We may find, too, surveyed right-angled Pythagorean triangles, in particular those containing sides with proportions 3:4:5. Perhaps we shall encounter an

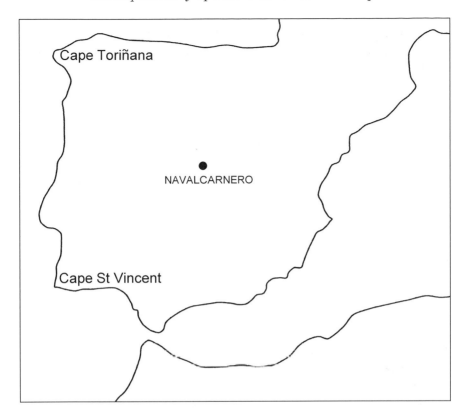

Navalcarnero, an *omphalos* at the centre of the Iberian Peninsula, equidistant from Cape Toriñana and Cape St Vincent.

omphalos, the central marker of a circumscribed territory, such as Navalcarnero (literally 'navel cairn') near Madrid in the Iberian Peninsula, equidistant from Cape Toriñana and Cape St Vincent. The original *omphalos* at Delphi was placed where the straight flight paths of two eagles (or doves) crossed each other (Lempriere, *Bibliotheca classica*). Common to many esoteric philosophies is the concept of liminality that, among other notions of transition, is concerned with thresholds and boundaries. Movement across liminal boundaries must be performed in prescribed fashion and at 'special' places. In addition to these features (and the list is not exhausted by it) we may find that place-names are descriptive of their symbolic importance, as with Navalcarnero.

The Pythagoreans were also preoccupied with the symbolism suggested by the relative proportions of the human body, as illustrated by Leonardo da Vinci's Vitruvian man, named after the first-century Roman architect

Vitruvius who gave the supposed relative size of a part of the body in terms of other parts; for example, a cubit is the width of six palms, and a man's height is four cubits; it is also the length of ten hands. The factors involved are always whole numbers, and sometimes do not provide a good description of a typical body. Vitruvius also wrote that the proportions of a temple should reflect those of the human body. As we noted, Vincent Scully has shown just how ancient and widespread was mankind's perception of a symbolic landscape as sharing the human form. Perhaps Pythagorean landscapes possess similar general models.

Pythagoreans were also interested in the harmonies generated by plucked pairs of identical stretched strings, stopped at different intervals. Can we recover the sound of the spinning universe as they imagined hearing it?

What if?

Suppose we were to find a landscape pattern containing all or most of the principles discussed above; would we be justified in maintaining that it was purposefully man-made? Such complex spatial systems are not readily amenable to systematic probabilistic statistical analysis. There are those who claim that with so many natural and artificial elements inhabiting the landscape, one can impose whatever pattern one chooses; but this is not the case, as the best efforts of Michell and Maltwood, discussed previously, so clearly demonstrate. Purposefulness is deduced by the discovery of more patterns designed to the same model, and by consistent accuracy in surveying them. Accuracy in surveying must be matched by accuracy in analysis. For this study a computer program has been written that can measure distances on the globe to an accuracy of one metre and angles to within one hundredth of a degree of arc; it also computes the line of best fit through a set of quasi-linear points and displays the departure of every point from this average line.

Cosmology for beginners

Further discussion will include mention of the Precession of the Equinoxes ('precession'), and it is best to deal with the mechanics of the matter here.

It helps to imagine the spinning earth as located at the centre of a huge stationary sphere, on the inside of which the fixed stars are painted.

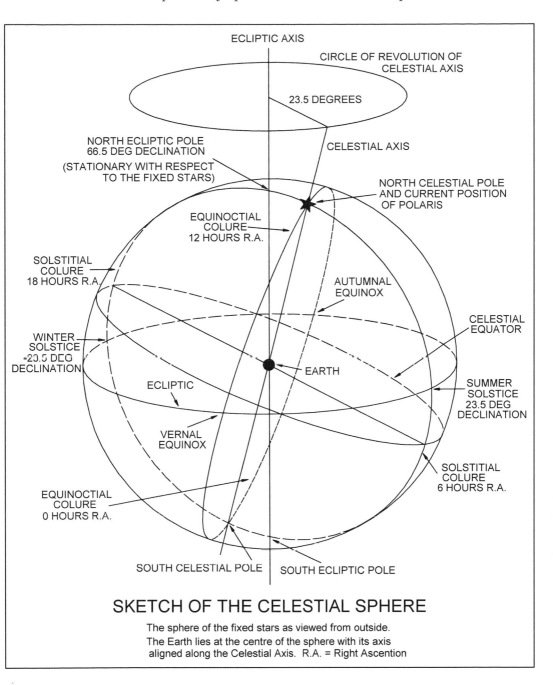

ECLIPTIC AXIS

CIRCLE OF REVOLUTION OF
CELESTIAL AXIS

23.5 DEGREES

NORTH ECLIPTIC POLE
66.5 DEG DECLINATION

CELESTIAL AXIS

(STATIONARY WITH RESPECT
TO THE FIXED STARS)

NORTH CELESTIAL POLE
AND CURRENT POSITION
OF POLARIS

EQUINOCTIAL
COLURE
12 HOURS R.A.

SOLSTITIAL
COLURE
18 HOURS R.A.

AUTUMNAL
EQUINOX

CELESTIAL
EQUATOR

WINTER
SOLSTICE
-23.5 DEG
DECLINATION

ECLIPTIC

EARTH

SUMMER
SOLSTICE
23.5 DEG
DECLINATION

VERNAL
EQUINOX

SOLSTITIAL
COLURE
6 HOURS R.A.

EQUINOCTIAL
COLURE
0 HOURS R.A.

SOUTH CELESTIAL POLE   SOUTH ECLIPTIC POLE

SKETCH OF THE CELESTIAL SPHERE

The sphere of the fixed stars as viewed from outside.
The Earth lies at the centre of the sphere with its axis
aligned along the Celestial Axis. R.A. = Right Ascention

The celestial equator is the great circle formed by the intersection of the plane of the earth's equator (extended into space) as it cuts the celestial sphere. Similarly, the celestial poles lie where the extended axis of the earth reaches the celestial sphere. The ecliptic is a great circle drawn on the celestial sphere marked out by the sun's position as it moves through the fixed stars over the course of a year. The earth's axis is tilted 66½ degrees to the plane of its orbit round the sun, which results in the progression of the seasons throughout the year. The value of the tilt accounts for the tropics (both terrestrial and celestial) being located 23½ degrees north and south of the terrestrial and celestial equators respectively, and for the plane of the ecliptic being angled at 23½ degrees to the plane of the celestial equator. However, the spinning earth wobbles like a gyroscope in motion so that over a period of about 26,000 years the celestial poles describe a circle on the canopy of the fixed stars with an angular radius of 23½ degrees.

Currently, the northern projection of the wobbling axis is aimed towards the star Polaris, but in 2,800 BC it pointed at Thuban, the alpha star of the constellation of Draco, the Dragon. These two stars, and the bright star Vega, all lie fortuitously close to 23½ degrees from the north ecliptic pole, and take turns to be the pole star. The north ecliptic pole lies at a declination of 66½ degrees, within Draco; no prominent star marks it. (Recall that declination on the celestial sphere is directly equivalent to latitude on the terrestrial one.) The axial wobble also causes the equinoctial points (where the sun crosses the celestial equator in spring and autumn) to move around the ecliptic through those constellations that lie athwart it, those of the Zodiac, in the course of a year; this movement applies to all points lying on the ecliptic, including the solstitial points, those where the sun is at its extreme angular distances (± 23½ degrees) from the celestial equator. It is this movement that is known as the Precession of the Equinoxes. It was described by the Greek astronomer Hipparchus of Rhodes in the second century BC; however, the consequences of precession would have been obvious to any culture that kept lengthy astronomical records, such as the Babylonians. The main point to bear in mind here is that the ecliptic poles, unlike the celestial ones, sensibly retain their positions with respect to the fixed stars for very long periods of time.

Lines that clothe the wold and meet the sky

It is a good idea to start with the concept of what constitutes an alignment. When William Mudge surveyed the baseline for the Ordnance Survey's mapping of England in 1794, he sighted from one end to the other. What was the nature of the line between the two points? It cannot be a straight line because the face of the earth is curved in two directions, being the surface of a near sphere.

Short 'straight lines', for the purpose of laying out buildings, say, can be produced by stretching a string tightly, but longer ones require a different technique. I arrange two straight poles, some distance apart, aligned in a chosen direction, and return to the one at the start of the line. You take a third pole and, under my visible direction, plant it in the ground beyond and in line with the first two. I meet you at the second pole having removed the first pole and hand it to you. We repeat the procedure many times. Imagine that we inhabit a hospitable earth with no oceans, and that we strike out in a north-easterly direction in the manner just described. Gradually, as our latitude increases, we veer more towards the east, and then accrue a southerly component in our travels. Somewhere in the southern hemisphere we momentarily move east before regaining a northerly constituent until, moving north-easterly again, we discover the point from which we started. We have traversed a great circle. Loosely defined, a great circle is the largest circle we can 'draw' on the globe. The equator, the ecliptic and meridians of longitude are examples of great circles.

However, should we wish to survey a line of latitude, this method will not do because we would want to maintain a due east or due west direction. We would need constantly to check our direction by some means to ensure accuracy. A surveyed line of latitude represents a great expenditure of effort, so finding one would be a discovery of great significance.

How can one tell whether a line is deliberately surveyed? The answer is that it is not always possible to do so. However, extreme accuracy of alignment, significant orientation, distances between points on the line occurring in integral multiples of a standard unit of distance, and coherence of theme or nomenclature are all useful indicators. We shall encounter all these properties, and every line will be evaluated on its merits or otherwise.

Supposing we accept the dictum that the sky provides the cue to spatial order, then the most likely lines that define that order are the ones that appear on the armillary sphere: the colures, the tropics, the celestial equator, and the ecliptic. The associated ritual sites might represent significant points on the sphere: the solstices, the equinoxes, the celestial poles, and the equinoctial poles.

Of course, lines and points do not exhaust the scope of symbolic landscapes. There are other dimensions to explore.

A Victorian imagined likeness of William Rufus, from *The Popular History of England*, 1862.

Return to Rufus

Let's briefly leave the heavens and the landscape and return to my opening theme of Rufus who, like his father William the Conqueror, was a foreign king in a foreign land. He continued his father's work of consolidating and extending his kingdom. Had he lived to see the fruit of his policies he would have earned a favourable reputation. Instead, he is remembered for his weaknesses and the manner of his dying. His problem was that he made enemies among the barons and the Church, trying to force change too rapidly, too far, and at their expense. He was also greedy.

Rufus' court lay at Winchester, awaiting a favourable wind for France. His brother Robert, Duke of Normandy, had mortgaged his duchy to William for a period of five years to finance his participation in the Crusades. Time was up; Robert was on his way home from Jerusalem, and Rufus intended to be there for the redemption of the mortgage. But William had arranged a similar mortgage with the Duke of Guienne, and the treasury at Winchester was swollen with money for that loan. However, much of the wealth had come from the Church. A major plank of Rufus' monetary policy, engineered by his financial minister Ranulf Flambard, was keeping vacant many endowed ecclesiastical positions. At his death, Rufus held unoccupied the archbishopric of Canterbury, the bishoprics of Winchester and Salisbury, and eleven abbacies – while drawing their revenues as *de facto* head. The danger for Rufus was that much of the money had come from endowments by his barons, particularly the Clare family. Gilbert Clare had a history of rebellion against Rufus.

However, the departure of the treasure ship to France was delayed by a slow-moving depression in the Bay of Biscay producing unfavourable winds, so Rufus went hunting in the New Forest while he waited for kinder winds, taking with him his younger brother Henry, his friend and protégé Robert Fitzhamon, the brothers Gilbert and Roger Clare, and the Norman knights William de Montfichet and William Breutil. Also in the party was Walter Tirel, lately arrived from France. Rumours of plots had been in the air for weeks, and Rufus knew that he faced the danger of assassination. The night was spent at Castle Malwood, where the anxious king suffered a nightmare in which he saw blood gush forth from his own body and blot out the sun's light. The morning brought a messenger, a monk who related another dream, of how Rufus tore apart the rood until, no longer able to bear the insult, it turned and felled him. Flames and smoke had then poured from Rufus' mouth, shutting out the light of the stars. Fitzhamon related the vision to the king who, aware that his friend was only trying to warn him of the impending danger, said, 'He is a monk and dreams like a monk.' He handed Fitzhamon a hundred shillings 'for the dreamer'.

Then, another monk arrived bearing a letter from Serlo, Abbot of St Peter's in Gloucestershire, a man sympathetic to the king, or at least averse to the crime of regicide. It carried details of yet another monkish dream in which the Virgin begged Christ to take pity on the English and to punish their wicked king. The previous day, the feast of its patron, the sermon at St Peter's had been delivered by Fulchard, Abbot of Shrewsbury. It included the words, 'The bow of God's vengeance is bent against the wicked. The arrow, swift to wound, is already drawn from the quiver. Soon will the blow be struck; but the man who is wise to mend will avoid it.' Hugh, Abbot of Cluny, and his chaplain made similar prophecies.

Everyone tried to warn Rufus that disaster would strike if he did not mend his ways – more specifically, if he did not desist from shipping the Church's money to France. But the king had other plans. Sir Walter Tirel was a newcomer, not part of the conspiracy. Rufus instructed him, probably offering

The dead Rufus, from Barnard's *History of England*, 1783.

bribes, to stay close to the king's person, and shoot without hesitation anyone bent on violence. But it did not work out that way. Tirel failed, most likely because the assassin turned out to be his own brother-in-law, Gilbert Clare, Earl of Tonbridge: he could not shoot him. Neither would Clare shoot Tirel, but he blamed him for Rufus' death, which was true in a way. An accident was reported. Tirel fled and carried the blame all his life, but on his deathbed, when he had nothing to lose except his soul, he still maintained his innocence.

This, then, is the drama of Canterton Glen, where the Rufus Stone stands, a confused mixture of history, tradition, legend and speculation, beloved by folklorists and fantasists, but despaired of by historians. Yet within this tangled tale lie the clues to discovering thrilling facts. First, though, we must explore more deeply the nature of pillars.

2

PILLARS: POINTERS TO THE SKY

By symbols is a man guided and commanded, made happy, made wretched.

Thomas Carlyle (*Sartor Resartus*)

Pillars of different kinds

Without wishing to contradict scholarly opinion, which is probably divided anyway, I can perceive four basic types of pillar in ancient Egypt.

There is the stele, an upright slab of inscribed stone used mainly for tombstones, boundary markers, or records of important events. The most famous is the Rosetta Stone, setting out a decree of Ptolemy V and relating to taxation and the running of temples. Its decipherment enabled the previously intractable hieroglyphic text to be read.

Secondly, the obelisk is a pillar with a pyramidal summit, the 'pyramidion', and dedicated to the god Ra. They were often erected in pairs within a temple complex. Some claim that the god was considered to reside in the obelisk. The obelisks of Egypt were stolen by European countries and re-erected in their own prestigious locations, the second largest (of thirteen) in Rome being that at the centre of St Peter's Square. It is curious that popes were so protective of this symbol of pagan religion and allowed it to continue in its present position. Perhaps they acknowledged the validity of a religion that existed long before their own was created. It is a politically dangerous act to repudiate ancient philosophies upon which so much of one's own depends.

Thirdly, there are pillars that are both symbolic and architecturally functional. Such pillars supported the roofs of temples, or architraves that resembled pergolas. Often they were naturalistic in style, the best known being those depicting the sedge papyrus, or the lotus, their capitals shaped as the plants' buds or open flowers. Scholars have identified over two dozen more species of foliage depicted.

The *djed* pillar occupies a totally different category. It is wholly symbolic and was functional only in myth. It is an ancient and frequently occurring symbol, one of a score or fewer, the subjects of amulets, that includes the *ankh*, the tall cross with a loop, symbolising eternal life, and the *tet*, known as the Girdle of Isis, which, with unselfconscious ambiguity, depicted both the uterus of the goddess and her girdle, and represented 'security'.

Often these symbols were combined in pairs; thus the name of a treasury scribe, Djed-honsef-ankh, combines the *djed* and the *ankh*; that of the pharaoh Tet-ankh-amen (or Tutankhamen) uses the *tet* and the *ankh*, and the name of the god Amun. The rules and significance of combinations are poorly understood. The *djed* and the *tet* are frequently depicted together: the notions of strength and security are complementary ones. They occur as alternating symbols in friezes on coffins and graphic funerary texts. The dado of Tutankhamen's sarcophagus consists of such alternating arrangements, both as single symbols and in pairs. This alternation of the *djed* with a female symbol provides it with an identity as a male one: the two are clearly complementary as well as synergistic.

The djed *in detail*

The *djed* was known to the Egyptians as the spine of Osiris, the ladder of Osiris, or, colloquially, as Pepi's ladder. E. A. Wallis Budge (*The Book of the Dead*) writes:

> In primitive times it was customary to place models of the Ladder of Osiris
> in the tombs, so that the souls of the dead might have the means whereby

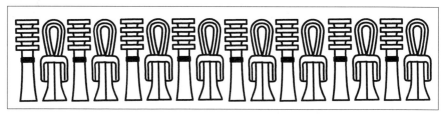

Alternation of *djed* and *tet* on Tutankhamen's sarcophagus.

they could ascend to heaven, provided that they were properly equipped with an adequate knowledge of the name of the ladder, and the words of power that were necessary to make it raise itself up and to stand firm.

The Book of the Dead prescribes the wearing of a *djed* amulet by the corpse so that it can 'enter into the realms of the dead, eat the food of Osiris, and be justified'.

Budge writes that 'the *djed* was in very primitive times the symbol of a god to which human sacrifices were offered, and the ground in front of it was "watered" with the blood of human beings'. He considered that it developed from the fused vertebrae forming the sacrum into an icon for the whole spine of Osiris. Can it be of surprise that 'sacrum' derives from the Latin for 'holy bone'? There are generally two depictions of the *djed*; one is very simple, like a baby's rattle, with a handle and four discs representing the spine. This is the version used for amulets and hieroglyphic texts; examples held in the hands of semi-anthropomorphic stone sarcophagus lids resemble objects that could have been turned in a lathe. The more elaborate version was often painted full-length on the underside of coffins; the mummy then lay on the *djed*, becoming 'an Osiris'. These elaborate examples of the *djed* show it with leaves and fruit, so it was clearly regarded as a Tree of Life.

Many scholars believe that the development of early Christianity was heavily influenced by the Osiris cult of Egypt. It is probable that the story of Jesus' birth in a stable was inserted into St Luke's Gospel by mythologers to ensure that Jesus had the correct credentials as an Osiris to enable his resurrection. Chapter 2 verse 7 of the gospel tells how Mary wrapped Jesus in swaddling clothes (strips of cloth) and laid him in a manger. For those who do not know what a manger is (the Archbishop of York referred to it as a 'drinking trough' in a radio broadcast in 2007), its name comes from the same root as the French for 'to eat', and it consisted – in one form, at least – of a V shaped container for hay, constructed by inserting two rows of slanting rods into a horizontal log: a perfect representation of a spine and rib cage. Gospel myth tells us that Jesus was, in effect, wrapped up like a mummy and laid on an image of Pepi's ladder in a sacred process normally reserved for the mummies of kings and priests of Egypt. The placement of Jesus in a manger also foretells (in retrospect, of course) his destiny to be eaten in the ritual of the mass.

My selected example of a *djed*, owned by the British Museum and on display there, is the one painted on the base of the mummy case of Itenib, who lived at Saqqara sometime after 664 BC (although far older specimens exist). It is

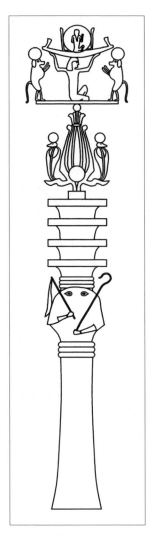

Sketch of Itenib's *djed*, on his coffin in the British Museum.

complex in form and impressive in appearance. The four-disc segment features (like the caduceus) two snakes, the *uraeuses*, forming a complex *atef* crown; above them is shown the disc of the rising sun containing an icon of Ra (signifying resurrection) in its barque, borne by Nun (personification of the primeval abyss) and flanked by the baboons of Thoth (the Greek Hermes, whose luminary is the moon and whose planet is Mercury). Thoth was the reckoner of time, scribe to the gods, judge of souls, the representative of the sun god Ra, a land surveyor, a mathematician, and male counterpart of the goddess Ma'at. However, the striking thing about Itenib's *djed* – and it occurs in other examples – is that the lower part consists of a shadowy depiction of a figure of human shape bearing the symbols of kingship: the crook and the flail. The image is wrapped in mummy cloths, but its arms are bare, and it is generally considered to be an image of the creator god Ptah.

To understand the development of the *djed* pillar we need to recall the myth of Osiris, the god of the underworld – and of much else. Osiris was induced by his wicked brother Set (who had already torn him apart in the past – only to be reassembled by Isis) to lie in a coffin. Set then threw the coffin into the Nile where currents bore it to the Phoenician coast, depositing it at the base of a tamarisk tree, which grew to enclose the coffin. The king of Byblos cut down the tree and used it as a pillar in his palace, but Isis returned it to Egypt. This episode accounts for the 'simple' *djed* pillar and was a myth of Upper Egypt. In about 2,900 BC, the pharaoh Menes united the kingdoms of Upper and Lower Egypt with his capital at Memphis. Ptah was originally a local god of Memphis. At first a craftsman god, he rose to the position of supreme creator god and was incorporated into the *djed* pillar. Some scholars claim that Ptah replaced Osiris in the *djed*, but the spine of Osiris is still present. There are thus two gods, or two forms of one god, 'within' the Tree of Life: the lower shadowy god and the upper god of access to the upper realm, the first of human form, but hidden, the second delineated by equally spaced vertebrae.

One thing that separates the *djed* from the other three types of pillar is that – apart from its use in hieroglyphic texts and cartouches, which mainly occur on walls – its image occurs as a horizontal feature although representative of a vertical object. The *djed* was raised up at the winter solstice during the festival of the god Seker, much as English maypoles were raised with proper ceremony at the start of May. The scholar R. T. Rundle Clark (*Myth and symbol in ancient Egypt*) writes that the *djed* is a world pillar, supporting the sky in the king's name, demonstrating his authority and guaranteeing his protection. If true, then a *djed* occurring in a symbolic landscape should run between national borders or, in the case of England, from coast to coast, over all the lands across which the king's writ runs.

I have usefully distinguished the *djed* from the obelisk on the grounds of shape, occurrence, and usage, but both are sun pillars, although arising from different traditions. To the ancient Egyptians, obelisks (a Greek term) were known as *tekhenu*, the word deriving from *tekh*, the name of the *ibis*, a symbol for Thoth. It is conjectured that the connection arose from the similarity of the word for the moon, *teku*, and consequently for a title of Thoth, *Tekuti*, the Measurer. Thoth, then, is the god of cosmic pillars, the supreme cartographer: if we found his pillar spanning the landscape of England, it would be measured out with perfect accuracy and would convey deep meaning. But what would such a pillar look like? What need we search for? Any obvious structure would have been identified long ago.

At the very least, an English landscape *djed* would require a shadowy, anthropoidal figure at its base; a stretch of readily identifiable spine above it; and a solar disc at its summit. It may also be orientated in the winter–summer solstice direction. This is a combination of features extremely unlikely to be formed by chance, so that if it were discovered, it would not be unreasonable to discover in addition other of the features discussed previously: an *omphalos*, cunning use made of natural features, mathematical relationships between distances, pertinent place names, and celestial correspondences. Perhaps, too, we would discover an absence of clutter or features that could be invoked to imply ambiguity – and hence chancy, fortuitous dispositions.

The reader should ask himself at this point what he would do if he found all these things – and more. Is it wise to try to open up the debate and risk the derision of 'wise' men and women, guardians of orthodoxy? Or is the prudent course to lie low, clutching the truth close, right into the grave, and preserve a quiet life? My choice is, I hope, the academically honest one. Knowledge, honestly gained, is rightfully the property of all mankind. It is a crime to bury the truth.

3

IN WHICH WE VISIT A PLAYHOUSE, PERHAPS THE GLOBE

To search with wand'ring quest a place foretold
Should be, and, by concurring signs, ere now
Created vast and round, a place of bliss
In the Purlieus of Heaven ...

John Milton (*Paradise Lost*)

Inter silvas quarrere verum
(To search for knowledge within the forest)
Motto of Brockenhurst County High School

What's in a name?

The Rufus Stone stands in Canterton Glen, at the heart of the New Forest. The place is a true glade, with a well-spaced mixture of oak and beech trees opening onto a sloping sward. The first mention of its name is in the Domesday survey of 1086 as 'Cantortun', where a Saxon named Chenna held half a virgate (about fifteen acres). Place-name specialists reject the notion that it was 'Chennaston', but they offer nothing more than the possibility that it was once the farm of the men from Kent, or that it refers to a 'rim' (exactly the opposite of the truth). If we look to the Latin of the Domesday Book, *'cantor'* could suggest 'the place of the bard'. Recalling that bards were one division of the Druids, we could imagine a hermit oracle living at this place, just as the sibylline oracle dwelt at Delphi and mounted the sacred tripod when she prophesied. There, grew a sacred tree; at Canterton stood a famous winter-budding oak, visited by Charles II and protectively empaled by his order. The

The first Rufus Stone, from the
Drivers' map of the New Forest, 1814.

parallels are persuasive, especially when we learn that the Rufus Stone was
three-sided, a sort of tripod, and crowned with a round ball. But there exists
an equally compulsive and convenient option. When St Paul (1 Corinthians
15:55) wrote 'O *Thanetos*, where is thy *kentron?*' – words now usually rendered
as 'O Death, where is thy sting?' – he used the Greek word that became our
'centre'. For the Greeks, it had more specific meanings: *kentron* was used for an
ox goad, javelin, or picket. The association of circle and picket suggests that the
kentron was the central stake to which was tied the rope by means of which the
surrounding circle was scribed. The similarity with a gnomon, which stands at
the centre of a circular sundial, is immediately apparent.

Canterton as a central point

Canterton seems to be linked with the idea of a well-marked centrality. In the
tradition of double meanings, the *kentron* explanation could be the prosaic one,
and the *cantor* one the poetic, thus reversing the usual perception of the Greeks
as being poetic while the Romans were pragmatic. This dual explanation
generates an interesting possibility that genuine mythological parallels existed
between the centre of Canterton and the oracle at Delphi.

Delphi is located on the southern slopes of Mount Parnassus, where a
round stone was deemed to mark the centre of the world. Recall that the myth
tells how Zeus loosed two eagles or doves from different places; they flew

in straight lines and Delphi was established where their two paths crossed. It may truly be said that Delphi is the model for *omphali*. Note particularly that the model *omphalos* lies at the crossing of two 'straight' lines. Another *omphalos* is clearly the Temple Mount of Jerusalem; medieval maps, which were often circular, featured Jerusalem as the centre. For Muslims, Mecca is the centre of the world, and they prostrate themselves radially towards it in prayer wherever they may be. The Great Pyramid at Giza in Lower Egypt is built at the geographical centre of that territory. Navalcarnero, as mentioned, is literally and physically the 'navel cairn' of the Iberian Peninsula. We can expect an authentic *omphalos* to have central connotations and its authority to be underscored by astronomical analogues and the intersection of straight lines.

Roman military encampments (however temporary) and many towns and cities were divided into quarters by roads joining opposite cardinal points of the compass, or approximately so; depending on the status of the encampment or garrison, the intersection was the site of the forum, the military headquarters or simply an altar. For example, the north-west corner of the forum at Roman Silchester (*Calleva Atrebatum*) is located at such an intersection. The primary north–south road was known as the *cardo maximus*, and the east–west one as the *decumanus maximus*. The eminent architectural historian Professor Joseph Rykwert, in *The idea of a town*, claims that all Romans knew their *cardo* represented a solar axis and their *decumanus* the path of the sun, and that their crossing was symbolic of the centre of the universe. The status of the Rufus

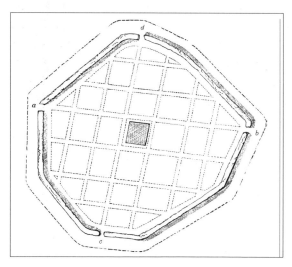

Roman Silchester, showing the four gates, the *cardo maximus*, the *decumanus maximus*, and the forum, from *The Popular History of England*, 1862. The word *cardo* is usually translated as 'pivot', but in astronomy it was the pole of the heavens, a point about which the stars revolved.

Stone as an *omphalos* will be confirmed if we discover that it does indeed lie at the intersection of a symbolic *cardo* and *decumanus*.

It was maintained that the earth goddess, Gaea, owned the *omphalos* of Delphi but that Apollo slew the oracle, named Pythia, and claimed the shrine as his own monument to the sun. Such mythological tales of killing and replacing are indicative of a change occurring in religion or in other esoteric philosophy.

Was Canterton originally occupied by a Druid sect owing allegiance to an earth goddess but then colonised by an authority whose major deity was the sun? It must remain an unanswered question, but we should remember that Druidic practices and beliefs lingered on in the Celtic remnants that survived the Saxon invasions, and in the Saxons themselves, who practised a religion based on gods and spirits believed to inhabit trees, rocks, rivers, and other natural features.

If Canterton was so symbolically important, it must have been used in some ritualistic manner. A mile to the north-west of the Rufus Stone lies a place known as Wittensford, where a track crosses a stream. It owes its name to the route taken by members of the Witan on the way to their assembly. The *witena gemot*, 'the meeting of the wise', was a political feature of Saxon society. Under King Athelstan, who was crowned in AD 925, the Witan developed into a major council of state. Before then, Witans were mostly local gatherings to settle land claims and other regional issues.

The nearest recorded Witan to the Rufus Stone was held in AD 931 at East Wellow, five miles distant. This is too far from Wittensford for the name to refer to that gathering. The Witan of Wittensford must have met close to that place. Canterton Glen is situated one mile from Wittensford. The ground surrounding the Rufus Stone is fully suited to a large gathering, as well as fitting the description of a temple glade. There is a well-placed natural knoll that would have given 'podium status' to the prominent men, one of whom was always a priest. So far as the existing evidence allows, the identification of the Rufus Stone as marking a Witan Moot is not unreasonable and more than plausible. While the correctness of this conclusion is not crucial to any argument, it does lend support to the notion that regular tribal meetings took place there over a span of perhaps hundreds of years because it was a symbolically important place. There is also a practical dimension for a religious designation. Often, discussions become disputes that lead to violence; the risk of physical violence is reduced when the opponents are standing on holy ground and facing spiritual sanctions for any transgressions of the 'house rules'.

The story as it is told

At some point, if we are to sleep soundly, we shall need to confront the question 'Is Canterton really an omphalos?', and supply a definite answer. For now, we shall move forwards in time and glean what evidence we can for the importance of Canterton Glen from happenings over two hundred and sixty years ago.

John Delawar, Chief Warden of the Forest, erected the Rufus Stone in 1745, a stone pillar about five feet high, of triangular cross-section and crowned with a ball. The inscriptions on its three faces were as follows:

1. Here stood the Oak Tree on which an Arrow shot by Sir Walter Tyrrel at a stag glanc'd and struck King William the 2nd surnam'd Rufus in the Breast of which he instantly died on the 2nd day of August A.D. 1100.

2. King William the 2nd surnamed Rufus being slain as is before related was laid in a Cart belonging to Purkess, and drawn from thence to Winchester and buried in the Cathedral Church of that city A.D. 1143.

3. That where an Event so memorable had happened might not be hereafter unknown, this Stone was set up by John Lord Delawar who has seen the Tree growing in this place.

This information comes from an article in the *Gentleman's Magazine* of 1789 by J. Milner, who wrote:

At the distance of a bow-shot from the column is the cottage of Purkess, a petty farmer, the lineal descendant of the person mentioned in the inscription, who conveyed the royal corpse to this city in his coal-cart. There are others of the same family in the parish, who will follow the occupation of their celebrated ancestor, that of charcoal making. I have learned from one Richard Pierce, an old man above the age of fourscore, now an inhabitant of this city, that he remembers his maternal grandfather, who was a Purkess, having in his possession the identical axletree, made of yew, which belonged to the foresaid cart, but which in a fit of anger, on its falling accidentally upon his toes, he reduced it to a bag of charcoal.

The Duke of Gloucester who, when serving as a New Forest Ranger, had tried to buy the axle from Pierce, and was much put out by Pierce's destruction of it.

Over the years, many of the visitors to the Rufus Stone took home their own souvenirs. The ball disappeared; the inscriptions were worn away; and the removal of many small chippings produced a slightly tapering shape. In 1841, William Sturges Bourne, Lord Warden of the New Forest, encased the old stone in a cast iron coffin. It, too, is three-sided and bears the same inscriptions, except that John is now 'Lord Delaware', and the two words 'had happened' on side three were accidentally omitted. A small grating was placed at the top of the column, so that visitors could view the original stone. But visitors poked gravel down the grating and the stone became obscured. Probings by the Deputy Surveyor of the Forest in recent years suggest that the old stone is absent from the interior, in line with the rumour that Canadian soldiers, who were stationed in the area, stole it in 1944, leaving a packet of Lucky Strike cigarettes in its place.

How true?

Tradition alone places Rufus' death here in Canterton Glen; documentary evidence does not exist. A claim has been made in recent years that Rufus was killed in the southern part of the New Forest. The historian William of Malmsbury, writing forty years after the event, describes Rufus as shading his eyes against the setting sun when the arrow struck. His brother Henry, in company with his friends, then galloped to Winchester, arriving before nightfall to claim the crown and the treasury. This journey could not have been performed in the time allowed from the south of the Forest. From the north, the journey would have been about seventeen miles – just possible with good horses and serviceable trackways. But the exact spot where Rufus fell is immaterial to the present discussion.

The legend of the charcoal burner Purkis finding the king's body and conveying it to Winchester dates from a later time, but it has become part of 'history' now. It has been embellished with the detail of the cart being turned away from Romsey Abbey by the abbess on its journey. There is something decidedly fishy about Purkis (or Purkess). It is a matter of historic fact that a Purkess lived in Canterton Glen in the nineteenth century. Another, John Purkess lived at Minstead, dying there in 1680; records show him to have been a charcoal burner. Trades persist within families, and he could have been the model for the legendary Purkis. Charcoal manufacture was a hard and dirty business, involving the building and tending of a large, turf-covered heap

The headstone of John Purkess of Minstead, charcoal burner. The inscription reads: 'Here lyeth the body of John Purkess who died Nov the 9th Anno 1680'. (*Author's image*)

of boughs kept burning with a restricted supply of air. The charcoal burner often lived the while in a temporary hut, also turf-covered. When the railways spread across England in the nineteenth century, distributing their loads of pit-coal to the towns, the charcoal industry declined rapidly. Then it was that the charcoal burner gave away his name, for until that time he had been called what his rival became known as – the Coalman. Purkis of legend would have been called Coalman Purkis, translated as 'Purkis the charcoal burner'. But the Rufus Stone does not record his profession.

Legend has it that Rufus' fletcher, one Cobb from Eling, handed him six new arrows before the fatal hunting expedition. On every one of the three faces of the present Rufus Stone is a pair of crossed arrows, making six in all. But a pair of crossed arrows is the symbol of the ancient Egyptian goddess Net (or Nut), the divine mother, identified by the ancient Greeks as the goddess Artemis. Net personified the place of the rising sun. 'Net' is the meaning of the Latin word 'cancer', the name of the northern tropic, so it is permissible to connect the goddess with the rising midsummer's sun. And there was indeed a Cobb the Smith from Eling who was granted the nearby estate of Rushington by Henry II in 1159 for the service of providing either 50 or 100 barbed arrows for hunting when the king should cross the bridge at Redbridge towards the New Forest. This service was reckoned to be an ancient one. But is not 'cob' a name for the hazel nut, a symbol of arcane wisdom?

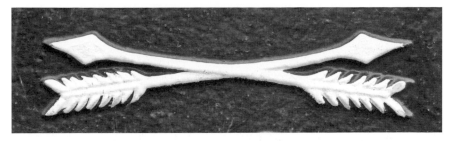

A pair of crossed arrows from the Rufus Stone. (*Author's image*)

The emergence of a shadowy myth-maker

At this point, a cautious researcher should smell a rat. Someone clever and well educated appears to have constructed a consistent body of 'legend' that could lead the unwary historian into assertions liable to prove his undoing. Rufus, it seems, has been deliberately employed as a tease and a decoy to the real nature of the Rufus Stone. Who would have done such a thing?

Irish hagiographics are full of references to saints named Colman. 'Colman' appears to be a saintly title rather than a personal name. For instance, it was a Colman who represented the Celtic Church at the Synod of Whitby in 663/64. Celtic was a language that underwent a major division. Linguistic scholars differentiate between p-Celtic and q-Celtic, because one letter replaces the other in the two forms. A good example is the word 'five': in Latin (a q-Celtic language) it is *quinque* while in Welsh (p-Celtic) it is *pump*. In parts of the great German wildwood where Christianity was but a Sunday religion, as late as the nineteenth century the name for the chief pagan god, equated with the Roman Jupiter or the Greek Zeus, was Perkos; in that regional theology, the god of thunderclap and lightning was indistinguishable from the oak tree in which he dwelt. 'Perkos' is the p-Celtic version of the Latin *quercus*, the word for the oak tree. Without trying too hard, a good translation from the Latin of Colman Purkis would be 'wise man of the oak' – the usually accepted translation for the word 'Druid'. Here, then, we have a nearly modern legend, in code, of a Druid living at the centre of the Canterton *omphalos*. Who invented these legends of Cobb and Purkis, and why?

Before attempting to answer that question, let's consider the opening thesis of Sir James Frazer in his *The golden bough*. Frazer postulated the widespread ancient ritual of the King of the Wood. At the centre of a sacred grove – Frazer's example is the grove of Diana the Huntress at Nemi, near Rome – dwelt a priest-king who had obtained his position by killing his predecessor and who maintained constant vigilance against would-be successors eager to kill him in turn. At the centre of the grove stood the sacred oak, and Frazer maintained that the King of the Wood was safe unless the oak tree became damaged. The similarity of these circumstances to the legendary position of Rufus is remarkable. At the centre of the sacred grove at Canterton stood an oak tree. Around it prowled King Rufus, a hunter, as was the mistress of the grove at Nemi. Rufus was anxiously trying to defeat a potential assassin. According to the legend on the Rufus Stone, the fatal arrow struck the oak tree before it lodged in the king's breast. The oak was damaged and the king was killed.

So great are the similarities of the two narratives that it must be concluded that the author of the Rufus legend was familiar with the myth of the sacred grove at Nemi, understood its significance, and crafted the Rufus story in imitation. This equivalence could only be sustained were Canterton indeed considered to be a sacred grove, and were Rufus deemed to have died there. Rufus as hunter was the embodiment of a mythological masculine hunter. The death of the king, perhaps cast as the icon of all mythical hunters, Orion, was fashioned into a ritual enactment of an ancient myth. Pierced through the heart, the king died. In a symbolic sense, then, Canterton, the place of the centre, is where the pierced heart of a god lies.

Down to earth

Let's repeat our experiment of surveying a line using sighting poles, this time beginning at the Rufus Stone and starting off in the direction of midsummer's sunrise. Off through the forest we plod, eventually arriving at Winchester Cathedral; only the fabric of that great pile prevents us from traversing the reputed (but disputed) grave of Rufus in the choir. Resisting the demands of fatigue, we skirt the cathedral and continue, eventually meeting Waltham Abbey, founded by King Harold II and legendarily the site of his burial.

This in itself is a remarkable discovery, but add to this the fact that Harold was killed on 'the knoll' at the Battle of Hastings, on exactly the same line of latitude as the Rufus Stone, and it becomes phenomenal. (Subsequent analysis of other significant sites on the line will show that it is truly a line of latitude. Recall that such a line is a *small* circle, so that if it represents a line on the armillary sphere it can only be one of the celestial tropics, the Arctic circle, or the Antarctic circle.)

An effigy of King Harold II, Waltham Abbey. (*Author's image, reproduced with the permission of the churchwardens of Waltham Abbey*)

History would have us believe that Rufus and Harold died on the same line of latitude *and* that they are buried on the same midsummer's sunrise line (at Winchester and Waltham respectively) that runs through the Rufus Stone, where Rufus was killed. This is a situation that is inherently improbable were chance alone involved. The probability of what history records happening at these points by accident is infinitesimally small. Was it all engineered to happen that way, then? Possibly. The sure facts are that Harold died on the knoll and that Rufus was buried at Winchester. Harold, or part of him, was probably buried at Waltham. But no one knows where Rufus died; only tradition tells us that it was at the site of the Rufus Stone. Let us make the reasonable conjecture that the line of latitude represents the tropic of Cancer, the declination where the sun stands at its summer solstice; then, it is quite feasible that Harold deliberately chose to fight on this propitious line. This supposition greatly reduces the chance probability of the pattern. If we now accept that Rufus' death was only said to have occurred at the site of Rufus Stone to enhance the symbolic symmetry of the death/burial pattern, the chance probability is further reduced. And if we accept now that the line in

Rufus' Tomb in Winchester Cathedral, from *Chambers' Book of Days*, 1864.

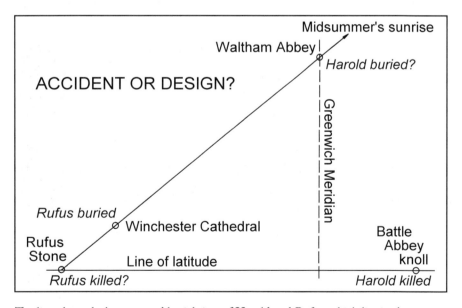

The line through the supposed burial sites of Harold and Rufus, which lies in the direction of the rising midsummer's sun, intersects the Rufus Stone, where legend suggests Rufus was killed. A line of latitude through this point cuts the spot where Harold was killed in battle. It is unrealistic to ascribe this pattern to chance.

the direction of the rising summer's sun is an analogue of a celestial meridian (probably the solstitial colure, owing to its azimuth) then the reason for kings being buried on it becomes a naturally symbolic one. With these suppositions and conjectures the immediate puzzle of the existence of a symmetrical death/ burial pattern is solved. Some authority has contrived to emphasise the image of an elementary armillary sphere projected onto the ground using two dead kings, one Saxon, the other Norman.

Let's hasten back to the Rufus Stone with our sighting poles to continue the line of the midsummer's sunrise in the opposite direction. Apart from an isolated cottage in the New Forest we discover nothing, until we reach the sea. The view is magnificent, for we stand at the highest point of the Dorset coastline, within an Iron Age 'hill fort' known as Flowers Barrow. If we could continue another seventeen miles into the English Channel in this direction we would find ourselves in grave peril, in the centre of the largest maritime whirlpool off the coast of Britain.

There are only two possibilities: we have discovered a deliberately surveyed example of the Cosmic Axis, Tree of Life or *djed* pillar; or history and geography have, by means unknown, contrived an accidental arrangement of facts and sites to persuade us mistakenly that the pattern was intentionally

Flowers Barrow, Dorset, seen from across Worbarrow Bay. (*Author's image*)

contrived. Sceptical souls who favour the latter explanation must be prepared to fortify energetically their position as more remarkable facts are unearthed and as analyses of them combine to demonstrate that their position is becoming increasingly untenable.

All carts lead to paradise

The legend of Rufus being transported to Winchester in a cart, and being turned away from Romsey Abbey for the night, is a homely version of a common and ancient myth of self-willed animals, of which I shall present six more. First, prompted by a recurrent dream, a farmer at Montacute in Somerset dug at the top of St Michael's Hill and discovered there a large stone that broke open to disclose a black flint crucifix. The cross was loaded onto a cart drawn by twelve red bulls and twelve white cows, but the team refused to move. The names of various shrines were recited; only when 'Waltham' was pronounced did the journey begin. At each random pause on the road miracles were performed. Finally Waltham was reached; there, the lord of the manor of Montacute erected an abbey worthy of the wondrous cross. On his last journey, from Stamford Bridge to Senlac, to fight for his kingdom at the Battle of Hastings in 1066, King Harold is said to have knelt before the cross, and as he did so it bowed to him. Waltham Abbey was home to an animated god.

A second myth tells how the first mosque was built where Mohammed's wandering camel stopped for a rest. Thirdly, the motif is found in the ancient Mediterranean world; the cities of Troy and Antioch both claimed to have been founded where sacred cows chose to lie down. Fourthly, in the Old Testament (1 Samuel 6), the Philistines watched the route taken by an unguided cart drawn by two cows, upon which vehicle they had placed the Ark of the Covenant.

The fifth of my legends concerns St Sebald. Sebald was a missionary to the pagan Teutons who died some time before 1070. Some claim that he was of Saxon origin. His name means 'Audacious Victory'; it must have been bestowed on him in old age, or even after his death, for in life he was a simple hermit. After death, it is said, Sebald's body was placed in the cart of a farmer; where the cart stopped of its own accord, Sebald had commanded his burial. His shrine is located in Nuremberg Church (sometimes referred to incorrectly as Nuremberg Cathedral). It was designed by Peter Vischer the Elder in 1488, and completed by him and his sons in 1510. Vischer travelled to Italy to refine the techniques he used in constructing the shrine, which is made of unpolished cast bronze; no doubt Vischer garnered some relevant esoteric symbolic motifs there, possibly gaining inspiration from the Scaligeri tombs in Verona.

Lastly, the cart myth belongs to St Kentigern, affectionately known as Mungo. Around the middle of the second century, Mungo visited the home of Fergus, a notable holy man. Fergus died that night, and Mungo placed his body on a cart drawn by two wild bulls, commanding them to stop at a place chosen by the Lord. The notable spot was named Glasgow, where a cathedral was built. We shall meet Kentigern later, when he becomes the vehicle of yet another common myth.

Whoever crafted the Rufus cart story was obviously aware of these legends and their meaning, and was trying to forge a direct equivalence with them. The clinching fact is the name of Purkis – Perkos – the title of the Teutonic god of the oak tree. A story from northern Bavaria has been purposely planted in the New Forest, has taken root, and flourished.

Cosmology in a nutshell

The study of Sebald's shrine yields fascinating information that will slot into place as this study progresses. It is based on a biblical model of the earth, itself deriving from ancient Egyptian beliefs, and is complex in its every aspect. A rectangular bronze plate sits upon a number of helical marine molluscs, indicating the surface of the earth floating on the primordial sea. At every corner of the rectangle (the four corners of the earth) sits a solar hero; Nimrod, Hercules and Sampson are instantly recognisable. Every hero guards a vertical bronze shaft, topped by a small sphere upon which an angelic figure holds an emblem and a candle. At the level of the spheres, the twelve apostles stand guard around the casket containing the bones of Sebald. All thirteen individuals thus reside at the apogee of heaven. Above the casket is an ornate representation of the celestial Holy City of Jerusalem. The shrine, then, clearly demonstrates, in the vertical dimension, the whole spectrum of the cosmos: the fundamental chaotic waters, the land of mortals supported by it, the pole of heaven, the abode of the saintly dead, and above all the domain of God, which cannot be entered by souls or spirits until the Day of Judgement. The shafts of the heroes provide the demarcation between the world of men and the abode of souls; they support the sky where there are points of light.

Sebald's shrine in Nuremberg Church, part of an engraving from *The Illustrated London News*, 1870.

A grand day out

Wednesday 2 August 2000 was the nine hundredth anniversary of the death of Rufus. The weather was fine and warm, the kind of day on which a man should take his wife to lunch at a cosy, quiet pub in the New Forest and then enjoy a walk in the woods. We drove to the Sir Walter Tyrrell, a short step from the Rufus Stone. We did not find a quiet pub. It was packed with members of the Tyrell family. Fortunately we found a table and partook of good food, which I washed down with a most excellent pint of Ringwood ale, 'King Rufus', brewed especially for the occasion. There, in red robes and a crown, sat Rufus on a bar stool, supping his last pint of the Ringwood Brewery's nectar. There, too, was Sir Walter, a mad monk, hunters and attendants. At the appointed hour we assembled on the sward outside, where *The Ballad of Red Rufus*, by Nick and Jeanie Mellersh, was enacted. Rufus died dramatically from an arrow shot by Sir Walter and was toted off to Winchester (there was a fingerpost to tell us so) in a two-wheeled cart, known appropriately as a 'Forest Truck', by a phlegmatic Purkis in wellies. Two hours later, and after another couple of 'last pints', Rufus repeated the performance, reinforcing the legend. It was all great fun. The English love dressing up and acting.

A scene from an enactment of *The Ballad of Red Rufus* by Nick and Jeanie Mellersh at Canterton on 2 August 2000. The dead Rufus is taken to Winchester. (*Author's image*)

There is more to drama than just fun, though. The medieval mystery plays and festal processions were as much about educating the illiterate masses about biblical stories as entertaining them. Drama can be serious stuff, especially when it glides into and mixes with ritual, as major services in the Greek Orthodox and Roman Catholic churches demonstrate. One obvious common element between secular theatrical performances and religious ceremonial is role-playing. The star actors and perhaps the extras, too, get a buzz from a successful performance. The audience gets a thrill. There are some dramatic productions, though, where everyone takes part in the action, where the audience is not aloof from involvement, where mere spectators are positively excluded. The rewards here are not the plaudits of the stalls and the circle but the sense of having participated in, of being enlarged by, the experience in some, perhaps inexplicable, way.

Master of the Rufus Stone

John de la Warr (1693–1766) came from a family ennobled in 1299, although the title once passed through the female line. Thomas de la Warr (1577–1618), the 12th baron, was the first governor of Virginia and is credited with founding that state. The Delaware River and Delaware Bay are named after him. His is the name of the first state, Delaware, to ratify the Constitution of the United States of America in 1787. As is by now well known, the founding families of the United States were wedded by the bond of Freemasonry. John was the 16th baron but not yet made an earl when he erected the Rufus Stone in 1745. The occasion was not conducted without ceremony – these events never were – but there is no open record of it. The stone marked a vastly important site in a scheme that, according to known Masonic claims, must be of central importance to Masonic philosophy. The ceremony was therefore, without a doubt, Masonic in nature. I shall reconstruct elements of that ceremony as it might have happened, just to bring out a few important points.

Interested parties

First, though, let's look at what the open literature tells us about Freemasonry. It is a fraternal and philanthropic organisation that disclaims the description 'secret society' preferring to be called 'a society with secrets'. Degrees are conferred upon members by participating in rituals that are based loosely on stories in the Old Testament of the Bible and allied sources. Prominent among these is the slaying of Hiram, the legendary architect of King Solomon's Temple. An often stated but obscure aim of Freemasonry is 'the rebuilding of the Temple of Solomon', and it is generally supposed that Freemasonry is concerned with astronomical symbolism and mythology too. Many of the old Bible stories are clearly of astronomical origin, derived from ancient myths of the Middle East (and perhaps beyond) that were current among the peoples who were neighbours of the Jews, who were conquered by them or who conquered them, and with whom they traded and intermarried. This astronomical basis of Freemasonry is confirmed in a work entitled *Ritual of the degree of the Noahites or Prussian Knights*, published by Reeves and Turner in 1812, which records:

> The true meaning then of the building of Solomon's Temple in Freemasonry is […] to the effect that the grand secret of all religion is this allegorical typification of the solar relations and planetary motions with mental and moral cultivation, and that such, in truth, is the lost secret of Freemasonry […] The Masonic building of Solomon's temple is the getting of a knowledge

of the celestial globe, knowing the mysteries of all the figures and grouping of stars on that globe: knowing further, that this globe is the foundation of all religion, knowing how to calculate the precession of equinoxes, the return of comets and eclipses, and all the planetary motions and astronomical relations of time […] The ancient priests thought that knowledge should be concealed from the multitude, or found profitable that it should be so: and hence our sacred and mysterious writings.

Of particular importance in Freemasonry is the figure of St John the Baptist, whose festal day is 24 June, described by Freemasons as midsummer's day, in contrast to the rest of the population who favour the day of the solstice, usually 21 or 22 June. The second coming of a patronal figure is a commonplace in mythology; Jesus and King Arthur are two well-known examples. Following a hidden formula ensures the second coming. For Freemasons, the formula comes from the New Testament (Matthew 3:3) which links the coming of St John with the passage from the prophet Isaiah (40:3) ordering his flock to prepare a straight path for the Lord, an instruction reiterated by John. Only for Freemasons, there was not just a second coming; St John 'came' annually with the rising of the midsummer's sun. St John the Baptist has always been associated with the sun in mythology. Freemasons, then, are concerned with straight lines of astronomical significance, with solstitial lines being of particular importance as representative of their 'patron saint'. Perhaps this is why some Freemasons, for example O. G. S. Crawford, the first Archaeological Officer of the Ordnance Survey, tried to ridicule those who seek an objective study of alignments. He asked the question: do they imagine the countryside to be mapped out with ruler and compasses? Well, yes, it appears sometimes to be the case.

A fantasy in Canterton Glen

A freely accessible American handbook of Freemasonry tells us that the covering of a Masonic Lodge is deemed to be the starry heavens, and Masons hope to arrive there with the aid of Jacob's Ladder, which he dreamed of as reaching from the ground to heaven. Let us imagine how this aspiration might have found expression in dramatic ritual.

Using his comfortable sinecure as Warden of the New Forest, John Delawar was able to arrange things discreetly. Proceedings were conducted in Canterton

Glen on the night and at the dawn of midsummer, more precisely 24 June, St John the Baptist's Day, 1745. The sylvan ceremony would make John Delawar a Supreme Artificer of the Eclectic and Profound Order of the Patriarch Jacob – or some such grandiloquent title.

Who was present and who conducted the initiation I do not know, but gathered together would have been members of influential families and perhaps minor royal patrons, some officiating, others as involved witnesses.

A small pit had been dug the day before, and workmen had positioned what was to become the Rufus Stone on its point of balance, lying partly over the pit. While it was still dark, John was laid on the ground, his head to the west and resting on the stone, probably wrapped in a shroud. Perhaps John maintained this state of vigil all night. He was dead – at least, in the symbolic sense that a Master Mason 'dies' and is 'reborn' at his making ritual. In this state John meditated on various matters philosophical and moral, and on the patron saint after whom he was named. At one point he was mentally attuned to existence as Jacob. He 'dreamed' of his ascent into heaven by means of a ladder, and he learned what he could of heavenly matters while he was there, primed by his earthly mentors. At a signal, he was summoned to arise, to be 'reborn'. This was around a quarter past three o'clock in the morning, and the trigger for this phase was the rising of the planet Venus over Winchester, which lay beyond the horizon, roughly to the north-east. Venus rose ahead of the midsummer's sun by an hour, sufficient to ensure its visibility in the brightening sky. The planet lay almost between the Earth and the sun and so was slenderly crescentic in appearance; that morning, within its crescent, Venus appeared to hold the planet Mercury. The Islamic symbol of the Star and the Crescent was created in the sky at this moment. This was a most rare configuration, and so a very special St John's Day.

Weighty words were uttered in the ritual and, as the Sun followed Venus and Mercury above the horizon, John tipped the stone into its upright position, perhaps aided by attendants. There followed an anointing ceremony in which consecrated oil was poured over the stone, just as the sun's rays struck the stone ball atop the pillar, an image of the solar disc, and an analogue of the round stone at Delphi. Being three-sided and capped by a stone ball, the Rufus Stone resembled, when viewed from above, the Masonic symbol of the all-seeing Eye of Horus within the triangle, which appears in Hermetic illustrations and as the Great Seal on the American dollar bill. The true significance of the 'Rufus Line' (the midsummer's sunrise line from the Rufus Stone to Winchester Cathedral) was revealed to him and John was given the grip, password and posture peculiar to his newly acquired degree. Canterton Glen was assigned an arcane name reflecting 'Beth-el', the name given by the patriarch Jacob to the place where he dreamed of the ladder reaching to heaven.

There then followed a re-enactment of the death of William II, whom Christopher Knight and Robert Lomas (*Uriel's machine*) claim was descended from a *Rex Deus* family, one purportedly tracing descent from the Zadokite priests of Jerusalem. The former part of the ceremony referred to the biblical concept of the solstitial colure. The succeeding part celebrated the establishment of the solstitial axis in Wessex. Rufus was 'slain', accompanied by an esoteric commentary laced with ancient allusions and moral adjurations. Just as Jacob, who was figuratively dead, made the journey to heaven up the ladder of the solstitial colure – as John Delawar had just done in ritual as well – the 'slain' Rufus made the journey from the Rufus Stone to Winchester along the symbolical colure in a cart led by a participant playing the role of the wise man of the oak, Colman Perkos. The body was said to sprinkle the Rufus Line with blood – blood from a slaughtered king of Zadokite descent, 'sanctifying' the axis in ancient fashion. The journey was not undertaken in full, of course. It would have been symbolic only. A short journey of a hundred yards, say, is not too far to sprinkle with blood; one could manage with a small cupful at most. It is also a 'journey' that can be made easily within the time-span of a dramatic ritual.

The cart had been provided by a local resident, Purkess, whose family retained its axle after the conveyance became worn out claiming, justly but only just, that it was the very one that had carried the dead Rufus to Winchester. Knowing the true provenance of the axle, old Purkess did not count it an ancient relic and was happy to dispose of this piece of inconvenient junk when in later years it unceremoniously fell on his toes.

From leaked accounts of the ritual, possibly by Purkess, the notion became popularly established that William II had been ritually killed at Canterton. In a sense he had been. The story of the cart is as speculative as the rest of my story, but it accounts for incidents in the legend. Research by Ronda Purkess into the Purkess family reveals that William Berkeley married Elizabeth de la Warr in 1466, and that the family of Purkess were retainers to the Berkeleys. At some time, the joke that their retainer, the grimy Coalman Purkis, was a Druid arose among the classically educated Berkeleys and Delawares, and was exploited in the ceremony in Canterton Glen.

The aim of this chronicle of the admittedly speculative events in Canterton Glen is to account for elements of the legends that have grown up around the Rufus story. The reader will have to judge their merits himself.

Winchester Cathedral, from *The Popular History of England*, 1862.

Where is the temple?

The Rufus Stone marks a point of huge esoteric significance, so why, unlike at Winchester and Waltham, is there no church in Canterton Glen? No definitive answer to this question exists, but the following facts may bear on the matter. Canterton is a 'Beth-el' site, an analogue of Jacob's resting place where he dreamed of the ladder to heaven. Genesis also tells us that God commanded Jacob to revisit Beth-el where he was instructed to change his name from Jacob to Israel. And that is about the extent of the Genesis narrative. However, the extra-biblical Book of Jubilees (32:21) expands on the story. It tells how an angel of God descended from heaven bearing seven tablets. One tablet commanded that no temple should be built at Beth-el. God had planned his Temple for Jerusalem.

In addition to 'Perkos' there exists another translation of the phrase 'of the oak', of which rich and educated men of the time would have been aware, and to which the Berkeleys and the Delawares may have wished to make a cryptic allusion. Pope Sixtus IV and his nephew, later Pope Julius II, came from the family of della Rovere, meaning 'of the oak'. Both were Franciscans, whose principal symbol was the oak leaf. Sixtus IV commissioned the Sistine Chapel from Giovanni dei Dolci in 1473; Julius II commissioned its ceiling, depicting the Last Judgement, from Michelangelo in 1508. They used the building as their own personal chapel. The art critic Waldemar Januszczak has spent thirty years researching the Sistine Chapel, concluding from its dimensions that it was built as an analogue of the Temple of Solomon, and that the two popes possessed an unshakable belief that they were to play leading roles in the fulfilment of scripture foretelling the end of the world.

Another conjunction

There is a wonderful precedent for John Delawar's interest in planetary conjunctions. Some planets can appear to stand still, even to turn around – relative to the fixed stars, that is. The fact that the earth and its companions orbit the sun in almost the same plane but at different speeds means that we can see loops and cusps in the tracks of the closer planets across the skies. Some Muslims take the year AD 570 to mark the birth of their Prophet, Mohammed. Note that in astrology, whose rules are not arbitrary even if its prognostications are, Venus is the planet that rules the constellation of Taurus. If you care to plot the track of Venus during that year, you will discover that it came to rest among the fixed stars when it lay between the horns of Taurus before turning round there, continuing briefly on the opposite course, and then resuming its original direction of orbit. The first reversal of motion occurred on the equivalent of 20 June, the day of the summer solstice that year, when Jupiter was almost coincident with the star Theta Virginis, and the crescent moon set shortly after sunset, close to Mercury, the messenger planet – all visible from Mecca. I do not know whether these facts are significant to any Muslims, but they do provide a wonderful allegory for the arrival on earth of Allah's Messenger and demonstrate the importance of planetary conjunctions to religious and esoteric philosophies.

4

A TOURIST'S GUIDE TO THE COSMIC AXIS AND THE HOLY WAY

Soon, the sun, on his refulgent path,
Will announce the morning.
Soon, superstition shall fade,
Soon, the wise man will be victorious.

Mozart (*The Magic Flute*, trans. Förster)

Step by step around the world I go

Let's start at the Portland Race and climb the Cosmic Axis (I shall prove its identity), carefully examining the sites on it as we go.

In the seas lapping Dorset lies the Isle of Portland, connected to the mainland by a narrow neck of land. Its southern tip is known as Portland Bill. It protrudes into the English Channel whose conflicting currents are deflected by the opposing faces of the Bill and focused offshore from its tip to produce the Portland Race, a whirlpool of great danger to seafarers, and one which has claimed many lives. The spectacle is at times awesome indeed, as if (in the words of *Hamlet's mill*) a plug had been removed from the ocean floor. The race develops about five hours before high tide and is most vigorous with a strong south-easterly wind. As a symbol of the primeval sea and its chaotic waters, we could find no better off our southern shores.

Moving north-westwards, we encounter the land, where stands Flowers Barrow. It dominates the cliff-top of Worbarrow Bay, where there is no other barrow of note. (A barrow is simply an earthwork, although the term is mostly used to denote a prehistoric burial mound.) The name of Flowers Barrow is obviously a modern one. Most likely the earthwork was known originally as

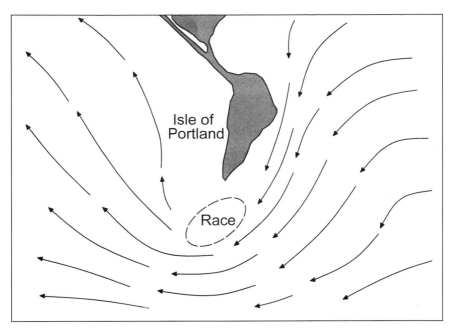

Sketch of the currents sometimes flowing round Portland Bill on the Dorset coast

Wor Barrow, the feature that named the bay, and its name changed to avoid confusion with a farm complex nearby that was given that one-word name. 'Wor' can be traced immediately to the Latin root *vor*; the Latin *vorago* means an abyss, chasm or whirlpool, while *vorator* means a devourer (compare 'voracious'). Both of these related senses accord with the notional rotation of an axis passing through the barrow. One expects a cosmic axis to rotate; symbolically the energy of rotation could derive from the whirlpool, but the reverse could be true, with the Portland Race being stirred up by the rotating cosmos.

Flowers Barrow is thought to date from the Iron Age, earlier than other features of the Cosmic Axis, which suggests that it controlled the placement of the Axis. Current archaeological opinion views Stonehenge as orientated towards the midwinter's sunset, which event the community assembled there to observe; perhaps Flowers Barrow had been constructed to perform a similar function in the Iron Age. The maritime horizon as seen from the barrow, which is about 500 feet above sea level, is consequentially nineteen miles distant; the centre of the Portland Race is about seventeen miles from the barrow. It is compelling to regard Flowers Barrow as a ritual enclosure where people

61

gathered on midwinter's day to watch the sun descend into the whirlpool on the horizon and be devoured by a sea dragon or whale. In the Old Testament book of Jonah, the whale represents the winter solstitial position. Jonah is an icon of the sun and is swallowed by the whale, remaining inside the animal for three days – the duration, for the ancients, of a solstitial sun. The myth of the sun being devoured at midwinter is very ancient. Perhaps, then, the surveyors of the Cosmic Axis used Flowers Barrow as a terrestrial origin, continuing the direction towards Winchester and beyond.

Moving on, we meet the remote cottage that we first encountered on our trip towards the coast. Why is it there? One answer could be that an earthen enclosure already existed, within which a squatter could erect an abode. If he did this within twenty-four hours he could, by law, claim title to the property. His frantic building of a partly prefabricated dwelling, aided by his friends, might just pass unnoticed by the authorities for a day. Whatever the reason for a cottage just here, we shall return yet again and stand amazed at the site's significance.

Circular arguments

The next stop is the familiar territory of the Rufus Stone to where, in folklore, the place of assassination of William II was moved from some unmarked and unknown location elsewhere in the New Forest for mythological purposes in a process termed 'status transference'. At a distance of 6561 yards due west from here, at Sloden, lies a rectangular earthwork named Churchyard whose low banks measure some 35 yards square. Again 6561 yards from the Rufus Stone, this time 36 degrees north of west, lies an exactly similar earthwork named Studley Castle. It is as if someone began to mark out a circle with ten equally spaced earthworks but the rest have been lost or not all completed. The notion of a circle is supported in some measure by the Knightwood Oak, nominally the oldest and largest oak tree in the New Forest. Its symbolic importance is such that Her Majesty Queen Elizabeth II, on Maundy Thursday 1979, planted a replacement for the decaying giant. Thursday is the day sacred to Thor, the god of the oak, and the weekday on which Rufus was killed. The Knightwood Oak lies 6561 yards from the Rufus Stone.

There exists that satisfying property of 6561: it is the square of 81, which is the square of 9, which is the square of 3. Perhaps this derivation is accidental; certainly its validity depends on the stability of the length of the yard over

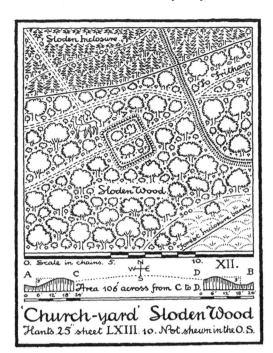

Sloden Earthwork (Churchyard) surveyed and drawn by Heywood Sumner for his *Ancient earthworks of the New Forest*, 1917.

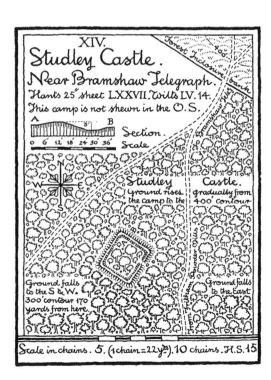

Studley Castle, surveyed and drawn by Heywood Sumner.

many hundreds of years. However, in its favour as a deliberate derivation is the fact that the square of 6561, in yards, is the circumference of the earth as measured by Eratosthenes, the librarian at Alexandria, around 250 BC. This immediately raises the possibility that circles of radii 6561, 81, 9 and 3 yards are 'world models' – circles that symbolically represent the earth itself – and that the 'Rufus Circle' is one of these. (The astute reader will have observed that I have moved from 'circumference' to 'radius'; the necessary factor of π will be discovered later.)

In the Great Hall at Winchester Castle ('Camelot' according to Sir Thomas Malory, the author of *Le Morte d'Arthur*) hangs the Round Table of King Arthur – or at least a copy of what it was supposed to resemble, made in the

An engraving of Arthur's Round Table, *c.* 1850. (*Author's collection*)

reign of Edward III. Originally it stood in Winchester Cathedral, on the midsummer's sunrise line, where it could be imagined to revolve as the Cosmic Axis was turned by the Portland Race. The associations of the table with time were recognised by the Tudors; in 1522, Henry VIII ordered it to be painted in an horal format of twenty-four sectors. In his twelfth-century romance *Quest of the Holy Grail*, Chrétien de Troys tells how Merlin constructed the Round Table with a hidden meaning, and how it reflected the circumference of the earth; in other words, why it was a world model. Indeed, it is the smallest such model possible.

Capital city

Winchester was a former Roman garrison built on the site of a town of the Belgae, the local Iron Age tribe conquered by the Romans. The first element of its name, 'win', is the same as 'vine', a plant that twists around, and 'win' carries the identical meaning. Later, the Saxons built a great minster there. St Swithin was buried close to it. When the Normans replaced the minster with a grand new cathedral, St Swithin's shrine was moved inside and became a great source of revenue: the greatest shrine in England until St Thomas à Becket's was built at Canterbury. Beneath the high altar of Winchester Cathedral lay a well dedicated to Apollo, the sun god. Winchester was once the capital city of England. We shall discover why that was. Meanwhile, after recalling the location of the Round Table here, we move yet further onwards and upwards to Waltham Abbey, the disputed gravesite of King Harold.

Easy lies the head

On the battlefield, Harold's head and one leg were severed from his body, which was left lying where it fell. William himself prevented further mutilation of the dead king. Harold's mistress, Edith Swan-neck, identified the corpse from 'secret marks', and the victorious William decreed that it should be buried 'by the sea'. There is a long tradition that it was interred in the Godwins' family church at Bosham, on the coast near Chichester. In 1954, during renewal works near the chancel arch of the church, a magnificent coffin was discovered. The skeleton inside lacked a skull and one thighbone, consistent with Harold's mutilations. The remains are almost certainly his. But the most recognisable part of any corpse is usually the head. Why was Harold's not recovered along with the rest of his remains? The answer must be that it was retrieved before the body, and taken elsewhere, most likely by one loyal to Harold.

The cult of the severed head was widespread among the Celts, and the notion that it was the repository of personal 'essence' persisted long afterwards. One need only refer to the legends of St Melor, whose youthful head spoke often after it was severed; Amesbury was a cult centre of St Melor in the late tenth century and its church is dedicated to St Mary and St Melor.

What would be the inspiration for interring Harold's head at Waltham? William did not allow Harold's burial at Winchester, alongside his father Earl Godwin, nor at any place likely to provide a rallying point for Saxon nationalism and resurgence. But Harold's head could have been taken to Waltham covertly, and for a very sound reason. His Nordic antecedents and chivalric upbringing ensured that Harold respected the myth of heroic warriors slain in battle being received into Valhalla, literally 'the hall of the slain warriors', where they feasted perpetually, enjoying the services of the Valkyries, maidens devoted to retrieving and ministering to the slain warriors. The name Waltham is usually taken to mean 'hamlet in (or by) the forest' but, in a system of deliberate ambiguity that is frequently encountered, its first element 'wal' means 'slain warrior'. In other words, by asserting that Harold was buried at Waltham Abbey, and possibly validating that assertion by placing his head there, someone was stating that the slain warrior-king qualified for entry into Valhalla and had been received there. Valhalla was paradise for the warriors, and the mythological entry to paradise, at least for heroes and kings, lies at a pole of the heavens.

Some authors claim that pillars carved with spirals represent spinning axes. Good examples exist in Durham Cathedral, Compton Martin Church and Rosslyn Chapel. The largest fluted pillar is that erected to the Roman Emperor Trajan; a spiral frieze tells the story of his first-century AD victory over the Dacians, and his statue once topped the pillar. Trajan is thus proclaimed lord of the spinning Cosmic Axis. Waltham Abbey has pillars carved with spiral flutes, thought once to have been inlaid with precious metal, appropriate to, if not exactly diagnostic of, Waltham Abbey lying on the Cosmic Axis. If the Abbey is an analogue of a heavenly pole, should the Cosmic Axis terminate here? We have already decided that if it is a *djed* it must run from coast to coast. Referring back to Itenib's *djed* reminds us that a considerable structure exists on top of the spinal element, so we had better follow through our journey.

Fluted pillars at Waltham
Abbey, Essex.

The top table

The sea is encountered at Lowestoft, at a spot known grandly as Lowestoft
Ness, a slight bump in the coastline, protected from erosion by the sea by
a breakwater of strewn rocks. It is renowned as the most easterly point of
Great Britain. The site is marked by a large, modern, circular tablet called the
Euroscope, set on the esplanade, which displays around its circumference the
direction of notable European towns and other features. The extended Cosmic
Axis goes plumb through its centre. If the *djed* must have a sun at its summit,
the Euroscope provides a suitable analogue. It is tempting to imagine that it
was added by some modern sage to complete the *djed*, but in reality it owes
its position to Lowestoft's just claim for the special position of the Ness.
However, the eastern bulge of England is under constant erosion by the sea,
and the Ness maintains its position only by being actively protected in a way
that adjacent areas were not. In other words, the unique property of the Ness
is an artificial construct, probably arising from a desire to impart a unique
property to the top of the *djed*; for it is highly unlikely that a line whose course
was set by the topography of southern England should cross the east coast at a
special point by chance.

Sunrise at Ness Point, Lowestoft – the most easterly point of the United Kingdom. (*Copyright Andrew Easton*)

The Holy Way

Having identified the sites on the Cosmic Axis, we must turn our attention to the supposed symbolic tropic of Cancer, that line of latitude passing through the site of the Battle of Hastings and the Rufus Stone. So much of the argument depends on the correct identification of this line that no doubt must be left concerning its authenticity.

We shall start at Battle, at a stone commemorating Harold's last stand. Westwards from this point, known as Senlac, the line eventually crosses the Southampton Water to pass through the old Saxon minster church of Eling, standing on its sandy knoll by the sea. (A minster church was in effect a small monastery with jurisdiction over the surrounding area.) The name 'Eling' is derived from the Saxon word *hlinc* meaning a sandy knoll by the sea; it is preserved in modern English as 'links', as in golf links, that phrase originating with the coastal golf course at St Andrews. Eling is simply 'Hele Hlinc', where 'hele' has affinity with the Hele Stone at Stonehenge, which marks the point of the just risen midsummer's sun, except that with Eling it is the equinoctial sun that rises due east. As with Senlac, Eling is clearly a name readily associated with the tropic of Cancer. Further westwards, the line intersects the Rufus Stone, and beyond that the small rectangular earthwork at Sloden, that is, Churchyard. We did, of course, register something extraordinary as we passed between Eling and Churchyard: the Rufus Stone divides the distance in proportion to the Golden Mean. Plato considered the Golden Mean to be a natural component of the cosmos, and discovering it in a system to be a sign of the divine mathematical mind in operation. Here, at the heart of the world model, lies Plato's touchstone.

Continuing on our way, the line passes over a conical hillock, Hallicks Hole Hill. Its name appears to derive from a Saxon-Celtic word pair meaning 'Holy Way' or 'Light Path'. The survival of such an ancient, factually descriptive name is paralleled by another hill nearby: Ragged Boys Hill. In Norman French, Raget Bois, the hill of the stunted trees, is a perfect description of the feature, where healthy root penetration of the soil is prevented by the formation of a dense iron-pan below the surface, resulting in underdeveloped vegetation.

Next, the line passes through a paddock on the edge of the New Forest named Paddis, which reflects the word 'path' in the language of the Jutes, cousins of the Saxons, who colonised this area following the departure of the Romans, and whose tribal name is discovered in the ancient name for the New Forest – Ytene. The Holy Way then cuts through the hamlet of Daggons, which the place-name specialists agree (for once) is connected with the Saxon god of day, Dag, who probably originated with the Philistine national god, Dagon, who functioned both as a corn god and a rain god. It is wholly reasonable that Dag should be encountered on the symbolic tropic of Cancer whose name here is partly of Saxon-Jutish origin.

From Daggons, the line cuts the southern terminal of that great Neolithic earthwork, the Dorset Cursus. This remarkable monument – parallel earthen banks stretching for six miles across chalk downland – was clearly once of immense ritual importance, for many round barrows and long barrows cluster about it. Ritual monuments have been located and excavated along its length (see Martin Green's *A landscape revealed*). It is not straight but has two doglegs. The directions of its component sections point towards extreme rising and setting points of the sun and the moon. It is inconceivable that the Holy Way cuts the southern terminal – which is marked by a Neolithic long barrow – by chance, which implies either that this point is the origin of the selected line of latitude that constitutes the Holy Way, or that the line predates the cursus. The common origin implies that they are linked philosophically, and confirms that the Holy Way, too, is connected with a significant rising point of the sun.

A report on the Dorset Cursus, by A. Penny and J. E. Wood in *The Archaeological Journal* recounts its alignments in detail. The authors describe the southern terminal, the Thickthorn terminal, as a carefully levelled platform. Such structures are invariably used for group activities, in this case most probably of a ritual nature. It so happens that a meridian that could justifiably be claimed as the central one of England (meeting the coast near Berwick-upon-Tweed) runs through the Thickthorn terminal. Its longitude is 2.0427 degrees west; the Ordnance Survey chooses two degrees west as its central meridian for Great Britain, only some three kilometres difference. The Thickthorn meridian originates on the highest contour on St Alban's Head. If the choice were a deliberate one, there is a case to be made for the group ritual activity at the Thickthorn terminal to be one celebrating the highest point in the sky of the sun: its crossing of the local meridian at noon at the summer's solstice.

At this point, it is unclear which came first, the Holy Way or the Dorset Cursus, but the evidence presented later suggests that they are at least early

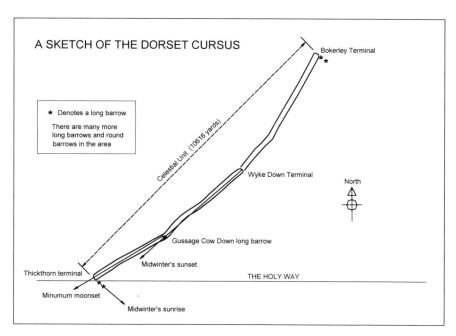

Constructed with data from a paper by A. Penny and J. E. Wood in *The Archaeological Journal*, volume 130, 1973.

contemporaries. A philosophy of life after death can be postulated for their dispositions. As the tropic of Cancer, the Holy Way is symbolically the highest point in the sky attained by the sun. By starting their journey on the Holy Way, souls progressing along the Dorset Cursus are deemed to be already at this highest point; further progression – increasing their declinations, in modern parlance – can only indicate that they are achieving yet greater status. I have found no way of calculating what point in the heaven is represented by the northern terminal, but logically it should signify the celestial north pole, for this is the highest point in the heavens that one can achieve. Human nature decrees that this honour was awarded to at least one Neolithic personage: he whose bones were laid within the long barrow at the northern terminal.

Beyond the Dorset Cursus, the Holy Way cuts through the church of St Andrew at the Dorset village of Lillington. Beyond this point it cannot be traced. Its extreme eastern end is the point of Dungeness.

Why a Holy Way?

Spiritual literature must include mention of such important ritual constructions as the Holy Way. The earliest allusion to a passageway of this type appears to be in the Egyptian *Book of the Dead*, a collection of pyramid and coffin inscriptions that codify the rituals necessary for the soul to reach heaven. Parts of this corpus could be as much as 7000 years old. Some of the inscriptions refer to the Royal Arch of the Sun, by which is meant the track taken by the sun across the skies in midsummer. From a practical point of view, how does one configure an analogue of such a track on the ground? Every point on it must exhibit the sun's maximal declination of 23½ degrees. The Holy Way does just that. The line I have called both the Holy Way and the tropic of Cancer is very likely to be the analogue of the Royal Arch of the Sun. Royalty seem to be scattered along it: Harold died on it; Rufus is said to have died on it; and Henry I drew his last breath on English soil on it.

It was from the quay at Eling on 1 August 1135, St Peter's Day, that Rufus' brother, then King Henry I, set sail for Normandy. The following day, the anniversary of his brother's assassination, he was asleep on board when the sun became eclipsed so that it looked like 'a moon three nights old'. A disaster was universally forecast. Henry never saw England again. He died on 1 December that year from 'a surfeit of lampreys' at the Castle of the Lions, Rouen. The lamprey, in common with the salmon, was symbolically a fish of knowledge.

The euphemism for the manner of his death is saying, simply, that he knew too much and paid the political price. In fact, the only total eclipse of the sun in AD 1135 occurred on 12 July. History has been twisted to agree with fact, as with the death of Eva Peron in 1952: Peronists falsified the hour of her death to coincide with that of her marriage to Juan Peron. These 'adjustments' are typical of the ones that 'history' has bequeathed to us.

The Old Testament of the Bible contains further documentary evidence for the concept of the Holy Way. In Isaiah (35:8–10) we learn that there exists a highway called the Way of Holiness; no lions or other dangerous beasts will threaten it; the path is forbidden to fools, but the redeemed shall return to Zion by means of it. In the Koran can be seen a similar passage in which Allah promises to guide his chosen people to a straight path, and that they shall abide in Paradise forever.

We have already noted the words of Isaiah (40:3) calling for a straight highway to be prepared in the desert for the Lord. To a seeker after wisdom, these words would appear as a direct order, a passage from a handbook of 'how to do it'. Seekers after wisdom expect their instructions to be cryptic: the more cryptic the greater their significance. The same expectation applies to addicts of cryptic crosswords: the more cryptic the clues the greater the sense of achievement for a successful solver.

The scriptural descriptions of the 'straight path' span the religions, a fact that indicates they are drawing on an earlier common tradition. From these passages we learn that access to the path is open only to those with knowledge and who are pure. The path leads to Paradise for the Muslims and to Zion for the Jews, Zion being for them the ultimate spiritual enclave. We also learn that if the line has a terrestrial analogue it cannot be the Zodiac, for its very name indicates that it is the circle of the animals, zoological constellations such as the Bull and the Ram, which are specifically excluded by the text from Isaiah. We are left with the tropic of Cancer.

The World Model

The creation of a world model in the New Forest makes two bold assertions: that Earth lies at the centre of the heavens, at the solstitial point, and that the monument in Canterton is the *omphalos* of the world, not just of southern England. The identification of the Rufus Circle as a world model relies on the numerical implications of its size and the existence of a well-marked terrestrial equator in the form of the Holy Way, which is equally recognisable as the celestial tropic of Cancer in its wider context. But there are other features that confirm the Rufus Circle as a world model.

First, the analogue of the sun shining on the model world can be identified as Eling Church for, recall, its name means 'sun marker hill', and it stands on the Holy Way at a distance from the Rufus Stone corresponding to the Golden Mean. However, in such realisations of the universe, the sun is never spoken of without mention being made of the moon: 'sun and moon' is the common phrase employed in ancient cosmologies and religions. If we can discover the model moon, there exists vastly more support for the model world argument. Where do we look for an icon of the moon? A satisfying view would be of the earth flanked by its sun and moon. Such symmetry demands an earthwork lying on the Holy Way, west of the Rufus Stone and the same distance from it as Eling Church.

The power and validity of any model lies in its ability to make successful predictions. I predicted that 'the moon' would be found at a specific location on Hale Common, a tract of open heathland lying within the New Forest National Park. The Hampshire County Council Archaeological Service obliged me with monument number 59938 in their Archaeological and Historic Building Record at the predicted position, tentatively (and rather desperately, I feel) identified as a medieval bee garden. But then, unlike me, the archaeologists have no basis to recognise it as a purely symbolic feature. The monument is a small, rectangular earthwork with its long axis lying north–south. Measuring its size from the top of its low banks yields the dimensions of 10 metres by 6.2 metres. In other words, the monument representing the moon is, so far as can be established, a Golden Rectangle. Suitably for the moon, which is associated in myth with water, a nearby spring discharges a small stream that runs along its northern edge.

In the diagram over the page, 'the moon' and other features fall on grid lines, which are explained fully in Chapter 6; they are lines used to survey the pattern being described. The grid line through 'the moon' is defined by the alignment through two ancient churches, Micheldever and Harbridge; their significance will emerge later.

The notion of a world model is also supported by the depiction of the terrestrial tropic of Capricorn. The assumption is made here that latitude within the world model is linearly distributed from north to south; given the primitive surveying techniques of the past, this is the only practical assumption. Within the model world lie three old churches: Bramshaw,

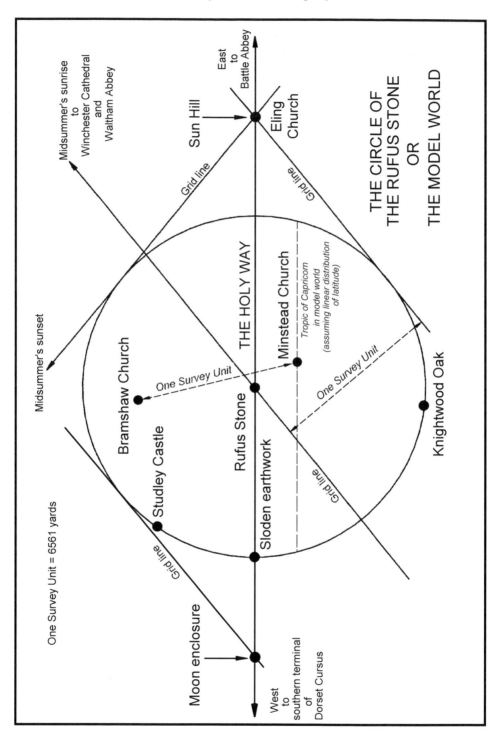

Minstead and Lyndhurst (although Lyndhurst was rebuilt in 1859). Bramshaw and Lyndhurst churches stand on hilltops, and it must be assumed that the elevated, prominent positions were what determined their locations. Until 1895, when county boundaries were moved, Bramshaw Church's nave lay in Wiltshire and its chancel in Hampshire, a supremely liminal situation. Since the locations of natural hills are independent of any pattern imposed by man on the landscape, neither Bramshaw nor Lyndhust churches were sited to mark significant points. In contrast, Minstead Church is situated on less featured ground; a surveyor possessed the freedom to locate it in a symbolically relevant position. But it stands 6561 yards from Bramshaw Church at a point 1724 yards to the south of the Holy Way. A line parallel to the Holy Way through this point represents a symbolic terrestrial latitude of 23.65 degrees south. This is a phenomenal result: the one old church available for location within the model world is sited on the model's tropic of Capricorn with the value appropriate for AD 300.

Bramshaw Church is dedicated to St Peter, who holds the keys to the heavens. Although constrained to his randomly placed hill, he nevertheless controls 'the world' for, through the standard measure of 6561 yards, he places Minstead Church to mark the tropic. This interpretation can be extended to assert that St Peter (or his successors, the popes) exerts dominion over the earth and, if correct, displays a hidden but vigorous element of Pythagorean philosophy present in ancient western Christianity.

Whose island?

We are now in a position to fit the landscape elements discussed so far into a standard model. In allegorical form, the Holy Way is a *decumanus* and the Cosmic Axis is a *cardo*, albeit an inclined one. Where they cross in Canterton Glen lies the symbolic centre of the world and hence, for the ancients, of the universe. Politically, the pattern is intended to state, in well-understood terms, that Britain is a Roman military enclave or colony. Joseph Rykwert (*The idea of a town*) has noted, regarding the *cardo* and the *decumanus*, that for the Romans the formal order of the universe could be reduced to two intersecting lines in one plane. This is remarkably efficient symbolism, but we need to examine finer detail.

5

THE TRUTH IN NUMBERS

And Sigurd the Bishop said,
'The old gods are not dead.
For the great Thor still reigns,
And among the Jarls and the Thanes
The old witchcraft is spread.'

Henry Wadsworth Longfellow
(*The Saga of King Olaf*)

Next, when you are describing
A shape, or sound, or tint
Don't state the matter plainly
But put it in a hint;
And learn to look at all things
With a sort of mental squint.

Lewis Carroll ('Poeta Fit, Non Nascitur')

Words of encouragement

Henry Wadsworth Longfellow and Lewis Carroll (Charles Lutwidge Dodgson) could not have been designed more differently. Longfellow wrote: 'Tell me in mournful numbers, / Life is but an eternal dream!' ('A psalm of life'). Lewis Carroll, author of *Alice in Wonderland*, was a mathematician by profession, but was every bit as imaginative and artistically creative as his older contemporary. Together they illustrate a modern problem. Britain is still the only country in the world where it is fashionable to declare an ignorance of mathematics and to insult mathematicians by calling them 'nerds'. Reader, if you have received a basic education in the three Rs, and can dispute your electricity bill or scrutinise your bank account, you will experience no problems in understanding the use of number in this chapter or elsewhere in this work.

Perhaps the situation is not so bad as when Tommaso Caccini attacked Galileo from the pulpit in 1614. Michael White (*Galileo: antichrist*) describes how Galileo believed that the universe could not be understood without a knowledge of mathematics, for that was the only way to describe it. Caccini regarded this statement as blasphemy, and countered with the generality that geometry belonged to the devil and that mathematicians were heretics. Following suit, if critics nowadays discover that the author of a disapproved work is a mathematician, they parade the fact as an automatic condemnation. To be competent at mathematics is, in some lamentable quarters, a disqualification to any other intellectual proficiency.

Before embarking on the exciting arithmetical analysis of what we have discovered so far, and proving its deliberate design far beyond any reasonable doubt, I shall review our progress up to this point.

An overview

A circle, which I claim to be a world model – specifically an image of the Earth – has been described as centred on the Rufus Stone. The diameter of this circle, extended eastwards to Eling Church, is divided by the Rufus Stone in the proportion of the Golden Mean. An earthwork lies a similar distance to the west. I have identified the church and the earthwork as analogues of the sun and the moon. The radius of the circle has, in yards, the value 6561, a 'special' number. I have described an arc of a great circle pointing in the direction of the midsummer's sunrise on which lie a small number of ritual or symbolic points with relevant name elements: Wor (vortex), Canter (centre), Win (turning), Wal (slain warrior). It conforms to a model of a Cosmic Axis, described independently by an academic (de Santillana) as originating in a maritime whirlpool. The same model postulates that the line is an analogue of the solstitial colure and that other lines from the armillary sphere may be present along with it. A line of latitude has been found, passing through the Rufus Stone, explicitly named the Holy Way, containing references to the sun (Senlac, Hele) and passing through ritual or symbolic sites (Eling Church, Churchyard, 'the Moon', the southern terminal of the Dorset Cursus, Lillington Church) that could serve as a representation of the tropic of Cancer. These two lines are now defined by the extraordinary disposition of the alleged death and burial sites of two kings: William II (Rufus) and Harold II. I have equated the two lines with the Roman *cardo* and *decumanus*, and also with the ancient Egyptian symbols of the *djed* and the *tet*; where they cross, at the Rufus Stone, is identified as the analogue of the solstitial point, where the sun stands on the tropic of Cancer at midsummer, and is a strong candidate for an *omphalos* location. Consequently, but not crucially, I suggest that the two Egyptian symbols used together, as on the sarcophagus of Tutankhamen, symbolise the sun in its strength, a symbolic attribute of the pharaoh, and the fertile union of the male and the female.

The identification of the Cosmic Axis with both the *djed* and the *cardo*, and of the Holy Way with the *tet* and the *decumanus*, designates the *cardo* as masculine and the *decumanus* as feminine. The Roman ritual sites located at their crossing can thus be explained as a consequence of generative fusion. The Romans' practice of sanctifying their settlements with symbolic lines, as with much else in their cultural package, can be ascribed to an Egyptian origin, but its reduction of the description of the universe to a simple cross, while possessing iconic shorthand appeal (hence its adoption by the Christian religion) limits numerical and geometrical analysis. Conversely, the *djed* displays a great deal of structure; it possesses the potential for great comparative analysis. I shall therefore concentrate on the Cosmic Axis in its earlier manifestation as the *djed*.

The measure of the man

Our western society has become so accustomed to counting using the number system to the base ten, of Arabic origin, that we often forget that other systems existed as cultural norms. There are faint echoes of these when we use the word 'dozen' and 'gross', from a system based on twelves and grosses (144) instead of the more familiar tens and hundreds. The French language preserves hints of a system based on twenties (scores) with *vingt-et-un* and *quatre-vingt*. Since the advent of personal computers, everyone has become aware of the utility of the binary system, where the base is two and the symbols are limited by convention to 0 and 1. In everyday use is the ancient Babylonian sexagesimal system, where the base is 60: in angular measure, there are sixty seconds to a minute and sixty minutes to a degree. Because (analogue) clocks employ angles to show the time, the Babylonian system is used by them too, with sixty seconds in a minute and sixty minutes in an hour.

We have discussed how 6561 can be expressed as 'three raised to the power eight'; in other words the figure can be rendered in the number system to the base three (in which the only symbols could be 0, 1, 2) as 10000. In a number system based on nine (symbols 0 to 8, say) it becomes 1000, while in a system based on 81 (with 81 different symbols) it is written as 100. Extending this argument to its absurd limit, we could work in base 6561 and simply write the number as 10, that is one lot of 6561 (in normal base ten parlance) and no additional units. From now on I promise not to show off and to work only in the familiar number system to the base ten. What I need to establish now is the nature of the *distance* 6561 yards.

The fifth-century BC Greek philosopher Protagoras – whose name means 'the first to publish' or '*I* said it first' – was the first of the Sophists and declared that 'man is the measure of all things'. In no sense did he imply *physical* measurement, but that quality exactly captures the philosophy of the Pythagoreans for whom human measure and proportion were paramount quantities. Suppose we take the height of a man or woman as the basic unit of measurement. It will have to be a particular human, an average one, or a typical one, for he/she needs to be 5 feet 5½ inches tall (more accurately, 5 feet 5.61 inches). Count this distance as a 'second', then a minute becomes 109.35 yards, and an hour 6561 yards. This is the distance (3.73 miles) that a fit human being can cover at a walking pace in an hour. Time and distance have been unified by this mathematical device, something that was not achieved again until the advent of Einstein's theory of general relativity. Also delightful is the fact that there exist features of England's countryside that are measured out according to the ancient Babylonian sexagesimal system.

The distance 6561 yards is found as a common unit of measurement in the emerging pattern, so I shall give it a name for convenience. Resisting esoteric references, it will be known as a Survey Unit, about as prosaic as can be. I shall name an additional unit a Celestial Unit; its length is one Survey Unit multiplied by the Golden Mean. It is the distance between the Rufus Stone and Eling Church, also the terminal-to-terminal length of the Dorset Cursus.

More circles

My certainty that the circle around the Rufus Stone is a deliberate artefact and not a chance occurrence is the result of more circles with the radius of a Survey Unit being discovered. I am once again relying for support on the notion of a *model*.

The pattern of Breamore Miz-Maze (and of many more).

In the Hampshire countryside, at Breamore, lies a turf maze, known as a miz-maze but more correctly described as a labyrinth as its convoluted path does not branch. Such mazes were once common features of the landscape. One famously lies in the chancel of Chârtres Cathedral, where it is known, as elsewhere, as the Road to Jerusalem. Legend has it that the Breamore maze was constructed by the monks of distant Breamore Priory who would perform penance for their sins by crawling to its centre on their hands and knees. Both Nunton Church and Homington Church lie 6561 yards from the maze, as does a spot named Paradise on the map. Paradise lies 6561 yards from Homington Church, while the Rockbourne Roman Villa, one of whose mosaic floors contains a square maze motif, lies 6561 yards from Paradise.

Measuring the djed

Part of the *djed* consisted of a spine. The normal human spine contains twenty-three typical vertebrae together with the smaller atlas vertebra. (The atlas bone is so-called because it supports the skull, as Atlas the Titan supported the universe: skull hence globe hence universe, in this case. The spine rests upon the sacral bone, 'sacral' because it was once regarded as sacred. I cannot discover the reason for the name; the notion that it was the part of an animal offered in sacrifice only begs the question.) Imprecisely, the spine could be considered to consist of 'twenty-three and a bit' vertebrae. Given that the sacrum is level with the navel, and that the head unquestionably rests at the top of the

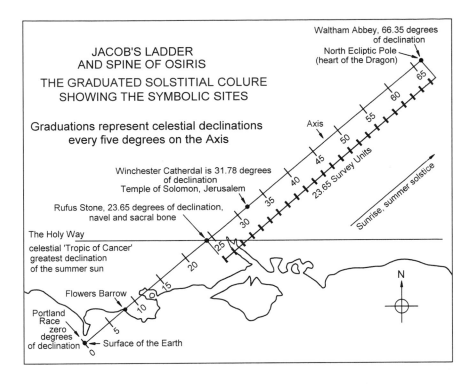

JACOB'S LADDER
AND SPINE OF OSIRIS

THE GRADUATED SOLSTITIAL COLURE
SHOWING THE SYMBOLIC SITES

Graduations represent celestial declinations
every five degrees on the Axis

Winchester Catherdal is 31.78 degrees
of declination
Temple of Solomon, Jerusalem

Rufus Stone, 23.65 degrees of declination,
navel and sacral bone

The Holy Way
celestial 'Tropic of Cancer'
greatest declination
of the summer sun

Flowers Barrow

Portland
Race
zero
degrees
of declination ← Surface of the Earth

Waltham Abbey, 66.35 degrees
of declination
North Ecliptic Pole
(heart of the Dragon)

Axis

23.65 Survey Units

Sunrise, summer solstice

N

spine, we might seek to find a correspondence in our symbolic landscape by measuring the distance between the Rufus Stone, an *omphalos*, and Waltham Abbey, the reputed repository of Harold's head. It measures 23.65 Survey Units. And 23.65 degrees was the declination of the tropic of Cancer in the year AD 300. The Ladder of Osiris was his spine; by climbing it the aspiring soul could reach heaven. The Rufus Stone is the centre of the earth; by climbing 23.65 Survey Units up the Cosmic Axis, the soul could reach Valhalla. Jacob's angels descended and ascended his ladder between heaven and earth. Thus, Jacob's Ladder is simply another manifestation of the Spine of Osiris. Metaphorically, when a man ascends Jacob's Ladder he seeks to attain a state of grace.

This undertaking is shown most graphically in a stained glass window depicting the liberal arts, a feature of Laon Cathedral in north-eastern France. Eight roundels of the rose window depict the liberal arts that were deemed essential for the education of an enlightened man: astronomy, music, rhetoric, geometry, and so forth. The central rose shows a seated image of Philosophy inviting the neophyte to ascend to full maturity by climbing the ladder reaching from her feet to her chin. The window has its roots in biblical philosophy, but

81

The image of Philosophy in Laon Cathedral, northern France.

displays a sharply secular edge, illustrating the notion of Renaissance Man, and with its doubly circular scheme reflecting the supposed rounded nature of one so fully educated.

Measuring the djed again

As astonishing as the fact that the Wessex *djed* exhibits a symbolic backbone – in accordance with ancient Egyptian custom – is that the human spine contains as many vertebrae as there are degrees in the declination of the tropic of Cancer. It is a very improbable chance occurrence. Could it really be a manifestation indicating that the cosmos is indeed designed according to anthropomorphic principles? The astute reader will now appreciate my little digression into the mathematical theory of the base of numbers. It may well be – but cannot be proved – that the ancient mathematician-philosophers chose the number 360, rather than any other number, by which to divide the circle into angles so as to achieve this result. The equivalence of the number of vertebrae and the solstitial declination could have been *engineered* to create the impression of an anthropomorphic cosmos. Below, we shall encounter another instance of mathematical skill being used to suggest the divine presence.

In this graduation, we have witnessed the expression of an esoteric symbolism, but we have also spoken in terms of an armillary sphere, which is a scientific model. Does the Cosmic Axis of Wessex, the solstitial colure, exhibit a graduation in degrees? Yes, is the answer, if we assume that Waltham Abbey represents the north ecliptic pole. We have identified the Rufus Stone as the solstitial point that in about AD 300 possessed a symbolic declination of 23.65 degrees. Then, the symbolic declination of Waltham Abbey would have been 66.35 degrees (that is, 23.65 degrees away from the celestial pole located at 90 degrees). The distance between the Rufus Stone and Waltham Abbey is 88.031 miles and the difference between their symbolic declinations is 42.70 degrees. We can use these figures to reconstruct a linear scale in the same way that we could reconstruct a school ruler if all but two marks on it were erased and we were told what lengths they both represented. A little arithmetic shows that the Cosmic Axis is graduated at 2.0616 miles per degree. This means that we can nominate any point on the Cosmic Axis and calculate what its symbolic declination is; alternatively, we could pinpoint a location on the Axis that represents a particular nominated symbolic declination.

Let's try this out. What point is the representation of zero degrees declination? The Portland Race is a large enough feature for the calculated zero declination always to lie firmly within it whenever it forms. The Cosmic Axis, then, does originate in a maritime whirlpool.

Zero declination is, of course, the value of the celestial equator. There is a sound practical reason for locating its analogue out to sea. I own a map of central Europe published in Moscow in 1809. It shows the longitude of that city (which increases in an easterly direction) as 55.5 degrees. Modern maps show it as lying 37.7 degrees east of the Greenwich Meridian, the internationally accepted meridian of zero longitude today. What is happening? My map uses longitude relative to a zero meridian through the Canary Islands, the western limits of the then known inhabited world, defined as such by Claudius Ptolomaeus (Ptolemy), the second-century AD geographer and cartographer.

This placement had the advantage that all the longitudes one wished to refer to were positive in value; all were longitudes east of the meridian. In precisely the same convenient way, all the symbolic declinations alluded to on the Cosmic Axis were thereby northerly. The Portland Race marked the celestial equator in numeric terms, but it also represented in esoteric parlance the boundary between the real world and what lay below the chaotic, primeval ocean.

Let's ask another question. What is the symbolic declination of the remote cottage in the New Forest? The answer, 20.23 degrees, is not a notable figure. A search of the skies as they were in AD 300 yields no star of any great magnitude lying there. What of Winchester Cathedral? The symbolic declination turns out to be 31.783 degrees. No prominent star with this declination lay on the solstitial colure or elsewhere within the time frame open to us. But was declination the intended measure? Perhaps the figure was intended to point to somewhere with a terrestrial latitude of 31.783 degrees. There is only one possibility. This is the latitude of Jerusalem; exactly, it is the latitude of Mount Moriah, the location of the Temple of Solomon. Winchester was clearly nominated as the holy and heavenly City of Jerusalem and its church built on the site of what became its minster as a revival of Solomon's Temple. Many historians of architecture claim that all cathedrals are analogues of the Heavenly Jerusalem. Christian Frost (*Time, space and order*) describes the processes whereby Salisbury Cathedral and its close were created as analogues of the Holy City. Certainly, where the Stations of the Cross – geographical points in the real, historic city – have been incised upon their walls, the intention is clear; but at Winchester the correspondence between cathedral and Jerusalem is supremely demonstrable numerically.

The accuracy of the latitude–declination equivalence is astonishing. Critics are apt to seize on such precision, arguing that it was unachievable in antiquity. However, the latitude of Mount Moriah, in the sexagesimal system of the ancient world, is almost exactly 31 degrees and 47 minutes, so by deriving the latitude to the nearest minute of arc (probably near the limit of their discrimination) the surveyors were, in this case, arriving at the exact value.

Why should anyone wish to establish 'Jerusalem' on the Tree of Life? The answer is that they were obediently creating the model described in the Book of Enoch, that enigmatic and suppressed codex full of astronomical lore. The Archangel Michael tells Enoch (24:5) that the Tree of Life will be transferred to the holy place, to the temple of the eternal Lord. This passage proves that the identification of Winchester with Jerusalem was not simply a local 'good idea', but was made in conformity with an internationally known and revered body of ancient wisdom.

This interpretation is too strong to challenge; however, due west of Solomon's Temple lies the traditional site of the Crucifixion, Golgotha, 'the place of a skull', its latitude the same as Solomon's Temple. Is there a notional skull at Winchester as well as at Waltham?

Vitruvian Man

Let's investigate an interesting correspondence, bearing in mind the familiar image of Vitruvian Man by Leonardo da Vinci and the biblical assertion that man and God are fashioned in the same image. Consider a particular bodily ratio. The distance from Flowers Barrow to Winchester Cathedral divided by the distance from Flowers Barrow to the Rufus Stone yields a ratio of 0.656. I am a normally proportioned man; standing, the height of my lips is 168 centimetres and the height of my navel is 111 centimetres. The ratio of these two numbers is 0.665. The two ratios are uncannily similar. Does Wessex possess its own Vitruvian Man? As before noted, it was the first-century Roman architect Vitruvius who wrote that the proportions of temples should reflect those of the human body, as we can see they do in some medieval cathedrals. So it is quite possible that Winchester Cathedral, or its old minster precursor, was meant to be identified as the mouthpiece of a creator God; that the Rufus Stone is his navel; and that Flowers Barrow is home to his feet. This conjecture will be securely confirmed later when other features of the body are discovered to lie in their correct anatomical positions; however, there is already enough data to justify a diligent analysis.

The symbolic declination of Flowers Barrow is about 8.1 degrees; one cannot be more precise at this stage of the argument because it is a large feature, some of which is lost to the ocean. However, using the symbolic declinations of the Rufus Stone and Winchester Cathedral, note that the numbers 8.13, 23.65 and 31.78 form a Fibonacci triplet, where the third term in a Fibonacci series is the value of the sum of the previous two terms. (I have chosen the exact value 8.13 to make this so.) In a system where every conceivable symbolic loading is employed, it is almost certain that this feature is not an accidental one. (The point on the ground that represents 8.13 degrees of symbolic declination lay within what was part of Flowers Barrow before it slumped towards the shore.) The principles that make the construction of this sequence possible, and deliver it a symbolic interpretation, will now be discussed in some detail. In view of my extraordinary claims, it is a necessary procedure, but the reader may prefer to take my word for it.

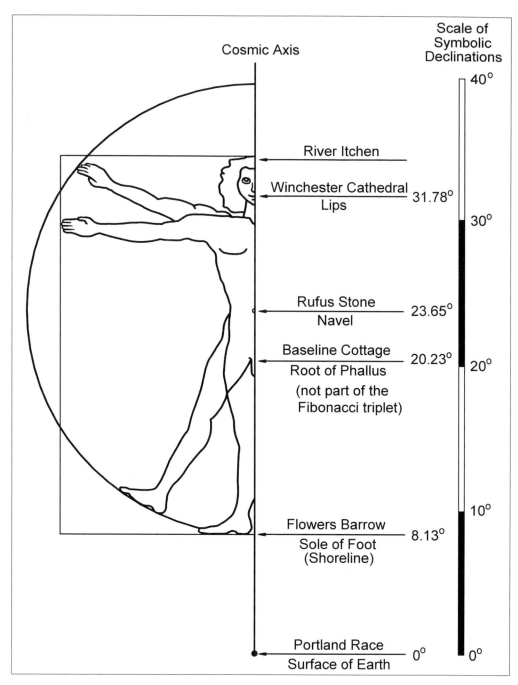

The image of Vitruvian Man, depicted in Leonardo da Vinci's familiar drawing, is here fitted to all the marked points on the Cosmic Axis between Flowers Barrow and Winchester. Note particularly that the Rufus Stone is confirmed as a navel by Leonardo's image.

Two important points arise from the Fibonacci triplet under observation. First, the rule for forming successive terms in the Fibonacci sequence dictates that the distance from the Portland Race to Flowers Barrow must be the same as the distance between the Rufus Stone and Winchester Cathedral – as indeed it is (alternatively, that Flowers Barrow bisects the distance between the Portland Race and the Rufus Stone – which it does not.) This is a general condition for any four points in a line to form a Fibonacci triplet as defined here. Secondly, the distance between Flowers Barrow and Winchester Cathedral, measured in degrees of symbolic declination, turns out to be 23.65. This fact should produce mixed feelings of awe and confusion in the alert reader – awe that it is the declination of the solstitial sun (a value that rightly belongs to the Rufus Stone) and confusion because Winchester Cathedral has already been assigned a different symbolic declination: 31.78. However, we have not discovered an alternative scheme for positioning ritual sites on to the Cosmic Axis; nor have we suddenly changed our origin (zero) from the Portland Race to Flowers Barrow; there is no suggestion that Winchester Cathedral is a solstitial point. What can be observed is the statement that the height of our Wessex Vitruvian Man – more accurately the height of his all-important lips – shall be deemed as defining 23.65 degrees. His bodily proportions are solstitial, and hence sacred, and fix the Cosmic Axis scaling of 2.0616 miles per degree that we have already discovered by argument and calculation. The discovery also vindicates the choice of 8.13 degrees as the nominal symbolic declination of Flowers Barrow, representing a vanished point within it.

The discovery of an anatomically correct Vitruvian Man based on a Fibonacci triplet with his navel located at a solstitial point and his lips at declination 31.78 degrees is, at first sight, miraculous. Does it mean that there is something magical about the numerical latitude of Jerusalem? The qualified answer is 'No', but that conclusion needs justification.

As with all bodily proportions, there is individual variation in the navel-lips ratio among a population. A casual survey of a few mature male friends yields a range from 0.649 to 0.676; Leonardo's Vitruvian Man has a ratio of 0.679. For a Vitruvian Man based on a Fibonacci triplet, there exists a simple formula relating the latitude of the lips (L) to the navel/lips ratio (R): $L = (2 - R) \times S$, where S is the value of the solstitial declination (here, 23.65). Plugging our extreme values for R (that is, 0.649 and 0.679) into this formula, we get permissible latitudes between 31.24 and 31.95. Jerusalem's latitude lies within this range, but it is not unique; we can design an anatomically correct Vitruvian Man with Fibonacci properties and a navel scaling to 23.65 degrees for anywhere lying within our rather narrow range of latitudes. This range translates to about one and a half miles in distance, but this liberty cannot be interpreted as an opportunity for chance positioning to occur.

How to do it? If, in imagination, we slide the Rufus Stone and Winchester Cathedral along the Cosmic Axis, while maintaining the distance between them, we shall create – together with the static pair, Portland Race and Flowers Barrow – a Fibonacci triplet wherever they stop, but for any particular latitude assigned to Winchester Cathedral (lying within the calculated limits) there will be only one stopping position where the new Rufus Stone scales to 23.65, and the Vitruvian Man thus created will exhibit a navel–lips ratio lying within mankind's normal range.

This is not the whole story. We have assumed that the surveyors had complete freedom (within the defined limits) to place the Rufus Stone and Winchester Cathedral where they needed to be to create the desired configuration, but instead, perhaps they had to fit their model to a previously designated location; maybe they had to accommodate an existing temple or church site, or an existing *omphalos* site. What constraints would they encounter if this were the case: is the task still possible while maintaining the other attributes? Winchester Cathedral is positioned in a most inappropriate location, on the edge of marshy ground; the Lady Chapel had been built on a raft of beech logs, and when these rotted parts of the building approached collapse in 1905. Only by a courageous and dedicated diver, William Walker, underpinning the structure with bags of concrete was it saved from disintegration. It does appear that the site of the cathedral was dictated not by its geological suitability to bear a large building but by symbolic demands. In contrast, the Rufus Stone appears as an intersection of the Cosmic Axis with a probably much more ancient line, the Holy Way; it most likely represents the fixed position that had to be worked into the system. Therefore, Winchester Cathedral probably owes its location to the position of the Rufus Stone. Since Winchester Cathedral had to lie 8.13 degrees from the Rufus Stone (to get the 31.78 value), Flowers Barrow had to lie 8.13 degrees from the Portland Race to achieve the Fibonacci triplet. The difference in symbolic declinations of Flowers Barrow and the Rufus Stone is 15.520 degrees and the mileage between them is 31.996; it was this particular calculation (31.996/15.520) that produced the scaling of the Cosmic Axis of 2.0616 miles per degree and determined the sites of Winchester Cathedral and Waltham Abbey. There is an element of luck here, though. Zero declination had to lie 16.761 miles from Flowers Barrow; fortunately this placed it somewhere within the Portland Race, which can at times measure several miles across, but there was no way of accurately measuring the distance of this notional point in the ocean, nor was there need to.

Far from being a chance alignment of points, Wessex's Vitruvian Man is seen to be a highly complex figure, based on known esoteric principles, whose creators understood how to resolve the mathematical issues associated with cramming at least four important symbolic features into an anatomically realistic 'statue' to produce a seemingly miraculous configuration, one that was designed to imply a divine assignment of the position of Jerusalem. But it was not simply a display of numerical and intellectual virtuosity. Vitruvian Man had work to do.

God the measurer

In the *Memphis Theology*, a corpus of Egyptian religious writings, the primordial mound emerged from the chaotic waters (Nun). The sun god created himself and stood upon this mound, thereby instituting the first sunrise and sunset. Flowers Barrow would be the last point of the local coast submerged by a massive rise in sea levels; reversing this calamity, it can be seen as a symbolic primeval mound, often identified at Memphis with the god Tatenen and with the solar Benben stone elsewhere. So, too, was the person of the creator a local choice; every town had its 'primeval mound', but it was first colonised by different aspects of the creator. As the creator god stood there, he uttered with his mouth the names of the things he wished to create, and thereby they came into existence. The process was named 'the operation of the Word'. The device was appropriated by the writer of St John's Gospel, the first verse of which reads: 'In the beginning was the Word, and the Word was with God, and the Word was God.'

Our Vitruvian Man is the shadowy figure of the creator god standing on his primeval mound at the base of the Wessex *djed*. This is such a momentous discovery that perhaps we should seek additional verification. The cottage in the woods, the only other site on the line south of Winchester, lies precisely where a normal man, projected onto the *djed*, would expect to find his crotch. It was bound to happen.

Several gods in ancient Egypt were depicted with erect phalluses, Geb and Min among them. They arose in different areas and at different times, but became compounded, in a confused way, later in the history of Egypt's syncretic religion. Geb was a husband and brother of Nut, their parents being the air god Shu and the water goddess Tefnut. Nut was the mother of many gods, including Isis, Osiris, Horus and Set; she was thus a fundamental character in the creation story. Nut was frequently portrayed in the 'all fours' position, her arched body, often arrayed with stars, representing the dome of the night sky: she was known as the Queen of Heaven. Under her lies Geb, ready for union with his sister-wife. Similar illustrations show a flaccid Geb with Shu holding Nut in her arched position; this configuration is interpreted as Shu creating, by physically separating Geb and Nut after the ritual copulation, the space between heaven and earth in which humans were created and dwell.

Min was another important ithyphallic fertility god, often represented by two sticks at right angles, consistent with the terrestrial Cosmic Axis bearing an attached skinny phallus; but Min was also closely associated with the constellation of Orion, the belt portraying his phallus. This is confirmed by the Arabic name for the belt, Mintaka (now reserved for its right star), which can be translated as 'Min's virility'. The symbolism behind the Survey Unit, the measure of the terrestrial Orion's belt, is thus made explicit.

Ghost of a survey

If we visit the enigmatic cottage and strike out precisely at right angles to the Cosmic Axis, in a generally north-westerly direction, at a distance of one Survey Unit we encounter the old church at Harbridge; another Survey Unit further on we are on marshy ground, at a place called Holy Head on Ordnance Survey maps; one more Survey Unit and we stand in Martin Church. From now on, I shall call the cottage Baseline Cottage and work on the reasonable assumption that a Survey Unit is the length of the god's erect phallus, a means of generation. I shall explore this Baseline in depth in the next chapter.

Some of the bodily proportions quoted by Vitruvius lead to odd-looking men, the problem being that the rules demand *integral* multiples (whole numbers) of other lengths. However, one rule Vitruvius did not state is that the height of a man is fourteen times the length of his rigid member. Searches on the Internet suggest that this is not too far from the truth; in fact, it can sometimes be correct. Taking the height of the god to be fourteen Survey Units conforms to the rule of integral multiples and leads to a well-proportioned figure; it places the crown of his head just north of the River Itchen.

Pi is discovered

We have identified the Golden Mean in our pattern, but can we find the esoteric number pi (π) too? The value of pi is defined as the ratio of the length of a circle's circumference to the length of its diameter. It was discussed by philosophers 4000 years ago, and its value disputed ever since, for it does not possess a computable value; like the Golden Mean it is a transcendental number, incapable of precise formulation in any number system either as a ratio of integers or as a string of digits. This property is one reason for its reputation as an esoteric number. Misguided individuals have computed the value of pi to many more than a billion digits, a numeric string that contains no recognisable repeating sequences. The ratio pi has multiple practical uses in architecture, surveying and engineering. For many purposes the value 3.141592654 serves well. For other less precise calculations, the easily remembered fraction 22/7 suffices; it provides a value of 3.142857143, an error of only some 0.04 per cent. For some ancient communities, 22/7 was regarded as the true value of pi. If our pattern is Pythagorean and all encompassing, where is pi?

The Golden Mean has been discovered in the way that the Rufus Stone divides the distance between Sloden Churchyard and Eling Church. It seems reasonable, then, that pi should be represented in the same fashion. We need to discover two clearly related line segments of 22 units and 7 units, Survey Units ideally. Such segments do not appear to exist. Where should we expect to find them? On the most important feature: the Cosmic Axis. But they are not there – or are they? Let's return to Vitruvian Man. His height is precisely 14 Survey Units. The only immediately observable esoteric relevance attaching to this number is the Pythagorean one that fourteen is the sum of the first three square numbers, 1 + 4 + 9, perhaps referring to the notion of the Trinity, common to many religions. Maybe so, but 22 divided by 7 yields the same result as 44 divided by 14, which is obtained from 22/7 by multiplying both numerator and denominator by two, a factor that cancels out when the division is performed. Since we already have a line segment 14 Survey Units in length, Vitruvian Man, the quest is to find a line segment on the Cosmic Axis with a length of 44 Survey Units.

Let's begin at Winchester Cathedral and follow the familiar ground to Waltham Abbey. Keeping to the great circle route we eventually hit the Suffolk coast at Lowestoft Ness, the most easterly point of Great Britain. The distance traversed is precisely 44 Survey Units.

That is an incredible result. England is transected by a midsummer's sunrise line (the Cosmic Axis) that stretches from a notable point on the

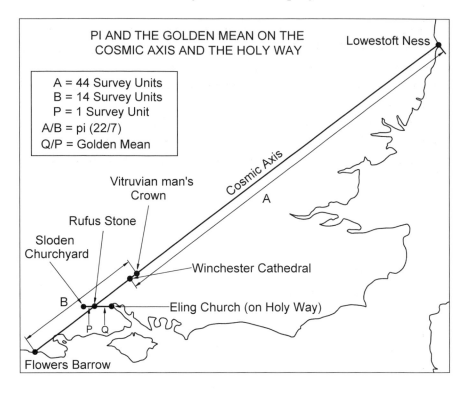

Dorset coast to a notable point on the Suffolk coast. It is divided into two overlapping line segments, marked internally by significant points (the crown of Vitruvian Man's head and Winchester Cathedral) whose lengths are both integral multiples of the Survey Unit and whose ratio yields the value of pi as recognised by early cultures.

The reason for the overlapping must be explored. Any continuous line (our coast-to-coast line included) can be divided into two separate, contiguous (non-overlapping) segments using the ratio of pi in two ways, one the mirror image of the other. It is improbable that either of the two segments will divide into integral multiples of any nominated unit; indeed, the probability that both should do so is infinitesimally small. However, the line can be divided into overlapping segments with the required ratio in an infinite number of ways, which provided the surveyors with what a mathematician would call an additional degree of freedom, which they used to employ line segments that are integral multiples of the Survey Unit. I can easily demonstrate that this is possible. Imagine a tube 14 inches long (or any other unit of length used consistently), free to slide easily within a second tube 44 inches long. By judicious sliding, this device can span completely any gap between 44 inches and 58 inches wide. With 'tubes' 14 and 44 Survey Units in length, the surveyor has spanned a coast-to-coast distance of 57.0847 Survey Units, yielding an overlap of 0.9123 Survey Units, or 3.4011 miles, which is the least theoretical overlap possible.

It would be reasonable to conclude that some symbolic significance attached to this stretch of overlap. If so, it would draw on the fact that it exactly covers the region of the skull containing the brain. If the mind of god lies anywhere it is here, mediating the value of pi.

The sound of Wessex

As part of their interest in proportion, the Pythagoreans studied identical, tensioned musical strings that yielded pleasantly harmonising notes when stopped in various integral ratios. Thus, vibrating strings stopped in the ratio of 4:3 produce a musical fourth, while those with a ratio of 3:2 yield a fifth. Kenneth Clark (*Leonardo da Vinci*), comments on the connection between Vitruvian Man and these harmonies, claiming that the notion of bodily ratios was of paramount importance to scholars in the Renaissance. For them, it was the basis of a philosophical scheme that complemented the Pythagorean musical scale, and provided a geometric definition of beauty. However, the two linked considerations of bodily proportion and harmony originated with the Pythagoreans, and 'men of the Renaissance' were only articulating their immense enthusiasm for the correspondence. The Pythagoreans would have been eager to know how the body of the Vitruvian Man of Wessex resonated, what relative frequencies it could be imaged to generate, what was the sound of god.

Let's make a scale model, conveniently about a yard in length, of the Cosmic Axis from the Portland Race to Winchester Cathedral (the god's lips, recall), and tension a musical string between these two points so that it vibrates with the frequency of middle C (C_4) when plucked. Stopping the string at the Rufus Stone (the navel) and plucking the lower part produces the note F_4, while stopping the string at Baseline Cottage (the crotch) yields G#4. A stop at Flowers Barrow (the soles of the feet) resonates at C6. Together, these notes form the chord of F minor.

Minor chords, as distinct from major ones, universally evoke feelings of mystery and melancholy. Francis Collins, a leading geneticist, head of the

Human Genome Project, describes in *The language of God* how the second movement of Beethoven's third symphony (the *Eroica*), which is written in the scale of C minor, generated a sense of awe and longing in him, a feeling of transportation into a spiritual dimension. One is left to conclude that this experience was at least partly responsible for his conversion from atheism to Christianity.

Tuning the model's string to middle C was an arbitrary choice, made to provide a concrete example. It showed that Wessex Man – and consequentially, the Cosmic Axis – conceptually issues a minor key harmony without specifying what key or pitch comprises the harmonic composition. The notion fits well with mathematics and religion, both of which are conceptualisations. Does mathematics exist independently of human intellect, or does mankind need to invent it? Is the same true for religion? Pythagoreans believed that both were manifestations of the mind of God. The minor key harmonic hum of the rotating cosmos surely formed part of their vision.

Philosophical ponderings

I have run out of superlative words, but it is extraordinarily amazing that so much information of astronomical and esoteric natures has been packed into a line defined by so few selected, surveyed points – four (the other three are givens). The only fortuitous topography is that the highest point on the Dorset coast lies in the midsummer's direction from the Portland Race, but even this coincidence is not so unexpected; the Portland Race is a large feature and when I have used the name to denote a point I have meant 'a point that produces the correct bearing lying within the large whirlpool'. However, the 'lucky' direction has been exploited to the full by the designers and surveyors of the Cosmic Axis with ruthless economy and consummate skill. Their names should stand alongside those of Leonardo, Galileo, Newton and Einstein.

The ancient surveyors and their legacy

We shall probably never know who these intellectuals were. I have called them Pythagoreans because the Cosmic Axis and the Holy Way exhibit mathematical properties consistent with their preoccupations; and they are the only known school of philosophy that could have designed such an image.

I have dramatically and freely written about Greek and Egyptian philosophy etched on the landscape of Roman Britain, but this is a valid thing to do. The Roman Empire provided a level of European internationalism under which scholars and ideas could move relatively unhindered by borders; the foreign postings of Roman soldiers and civil servants provided a neat mechanism for the interchange of different cultural ideas; and Egypt was part of the Roman Empire, having been conquered by Octavian in 30 BC. Trade, flourishing under the pax Romanus, also spread and interchanged ideas. Prior to the Romans, Alexander the Great conquered Egypt, in 332 BC, and the Ptolomies, 'Greek pharaohs', reigned from 305 BC. Alexander founded the city of Alexandria, famous for its library, which functioned as a university with up to 5000 international students; it was not destroyed completely until the late fourth century AD. The Greeks renamed the city of Khemennu 'Heliopolis' – Sun City; it became the chief centre of astronomical learning. The city of Khum they named Hermopolis, because they equated its chief god, Thoth, with their Hermes, the god of secret wisdom.

At some point in history, for some people, Thoth became known as Hermes Trismagistus, 'thrice majestic Hermes', who was credited by Hermetic writers of the Middle Ages as the author of sacred writings. These were supposed lost, but many alleged (and uninteresting) 'translations' circulate. However, there is one work, known as the Emerald Tablet, whose existence can be traced back to AD 800. It was translated by Isaac Newton, whose taste extended from mathematics to alchemy and astrology. It begins: 'That which is below is like that which is above and that which is above is like that which is below to do the miracles of one only thing.' The Emerald Tablet has been derided as a forgery, but once almost every sacred text was attributed to an unwitting prestigious character by its real author; in that sense, most of our sacred books are 'forgeries'. What the Emerald Tablet does, forgery or not, is to record a view existing before AD 800 that something miraculous could be achieved by marking out the ground according to the pattern of the heavens, and that such a pattern is associated with Thoth. Minds attuned to such ideas were at work in the first millennium. While such notions do not constitute evidence of construction, they are strong indicators of intent, and bite deeply into the weak 'inherently impossible' protest, which the eminent biologist Professor Richard Dawkins has famously dismissed as 'the argument of personal incredulity'.

On the matter of antiquity, the 'ancient Egyptian religion' was practised in Egypt under Roman rule until the fourth or fifth centuries AD. The Wessex *djed*, then, featured current, international sacred thinking, even if some of the symbolism employed was ancient in origin, just as the current British legal system is based in part on ancient Roman law.

It is fashionable to consider that the scientific view of the universe did not make headway until the Renaissance, but earlier brave and gifted individuals stand out, such as the thirteenth-century Franciscan friar Roger Bacon. Although the Cosmic Axis is founded on the 'magical' properties of numbers, it exhibits accurate and consistent measurements of both celestial declination and terrestrial latitude. By employing the ecliptic north pole – and not the celestial one – as the stable point in the heavens, it displays knowledge of the Precession of the Equinoxes, discussed in the first chapter. Indeed, it can be viewed as a declaration, perhaps a secret one, that precession is a recognised scientific fact, although perhaps as yet defying rational explanation. Here, then, may be the green shoots of enlightenment, the first tentative hint that mathematics was not just another expression of religious hocus-pocus but a powerful tool that would, with exertion and Inquisitional pain, eventually lead mankind into a sensible comprehension of his universe and assist in propelling him on a journey among the stars.

6

PAINTING BY NUMBERS

And those that were good shall be happy; they shall sit in a golden chair;
They shall splash at a ten-league canvas with brushes of comets' hair.
Rudyard Kipling ('When Earth's Last Picture is Painted')

The shadowy figure

As noted in the last chapter, different schools of Egyptian religion located in different cities had their own creator gods. For some it was Ptah, others Ra, and yet others, Thoth. As a mathematician and land surveyor, Thoth was a significant figure to the Pythagoreans. He, like Ptah, created things on behalf of the sun god Ra by speaking their names. He was known by many titles, including The Creator of the Heavens, The Counter of the Stars, and The Measurer of the Earth. There is every reason to suppose that it was Thoth who was imagined as supporting the Wessex *djed*. Thoth is needed because of his surveying skills, for with his 'measuring rod' of one Survey Unit in length he laid out a gigantic image of the constellation of Orion, nearly sixty miles in length, reaching over the counties of Hampshire, Dorset and Wiltshire.

When Orion is discovered, we shall need to answer the questions of why he is there at all and why he occupies that particular space. The answers will be that, within the grand scheme here unfolding in the Wessex countryside, he performs the same function as in the heavens, which is elaborated in sky-based mythology. We shall learn what this onerous task was.

Drawing representations of animals, objects and people on the landscape was once a common practice. The famous lines of Nasca are one example; nearer to home, the Cerne Abbas Giant rears his wicked head, displaying the

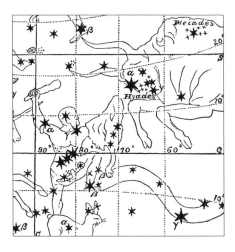

A depiction of the constellation of Orion as The Hunter, from Hugo Reid's *Elements of astronomy*, 1874.

weapons of lust and rage, instruments of domination. More peacefully, I have heard of a potter who baked a series of ceramic tiles, each one engraved with the geographical co-ordinates of its neighbours, and buried them individually in the New Forest to mark the outline of a huge giant. His motivation was that, although they were completely invisible, *he* knew they were there, so the giant really did exist; perhaps he felt that by keeping a secret that spanned the New Forest he was bonded with the land in an undefined but satisfying way unique to him.

Moving specifically to the representation of constellations, we can start with the issue of *New Scientist* for 16 December 1995 containing an article entitled 'Stars fell on Muggenburg' by Govert Schilling. It describes studies for the PhD dissertation by Linda Therkorn of the Institute of Prehistory at the University of Amsterdam. Schagen-Muggenburg lies about fifty kilometres north of Amsterdam, and there Therkorn found fifty-seven pits, about one metre wide and deep, that extended over some half a hectare. The pits traced the pattern of the constellations Taurus, Canis Major, Pegasus and Hercules. A typical constellation 'map' stretches for a hundred metres. Five hundred metres from the first group, Therkorn found a second, with an identical Taurus pattern. Animal remains in the pits provided a radiocarbon date of AD 350. The pits for Taurus (the Bull) all contained cattle bones; those mapping Pegasus held horse bones or teeth. Jawbones or complete skeletons of dogs were discovered in the pits of Canis Major. The Hercules pits contained artefacts like hammers and whetstones.

As confirmation of her thesis, Therkorn has found Pegasus and Taurus patterns at two other sites. One, dating from the first century AD, is at Uitgeest, thirty kilometres southwest of Muggenburg; the other is ten kilometres south of Uitgeest at Velserbroek. This latter site dates to the sixth century BC. Thus, the ritual practice of marking out constellations on the ground has been observed to exist over a period of nine centuries in the Netherlands. It must therefore have been of great significance and widely applied.

There are other ancient antecedents for buildings arranged in the patterns of stars. The Egyptian city of Hermopolis, sacred to the god Thoth, is said to have been modelled on the constellations of the Zodiac. Also, in the third century BC, the Chinese emperor Qin Shi Huang Di (who was buried with his more than 8000-strong terracotta army) constructed his palace buildings to the plan of the stars. No certain cultural connection with Europe can be claimed then, but the fact supports the idea of a widespread, natural appeal of such an arrangement.

The most convincing example of constellation mapping in Britain consists of three Neolithic henges at Thornborough in Yorkshire, each some 240 metres in diameter, whose banks had been covered with imported gypsum. They are arranged as a copy of Orion's belt. As confirmation of the intentional nature of the structure, the celestial constellation of Orion could be seen to rise through the southern entrances to the henges some 5000 years ago.

Thoth (or more correctly, his agents) was merely conducting a universal, time-honoured exercise when he used Wessex as a giant sketchpad for his portrait of Orion; but how did he do it?

How to map the stars

The Romans had accumulated hundreds of years' experience in surveying their colonies and provinces. Their methods and their high competency are well documented by Professor O. A. W. Dilke in his book *The Roman land surveyors*. Normally, the Romans marked out the ground in rectangles, a regular pattern of 'centuriation' forming a chequerboard, by which method the land was usually apportioned and taxed. They placed a stone at every intersection, numbered in a unique fashion. In north Italy, a system of squares with sides 20 *actus* long (about 2400 feet) is strikingly evident from aerial photographs. Rectangular centuriations are also obvious around Orange and Avignon. Apart from some very dubious examples near Rochester and Braintree, there is no evidence at all for centuriation in Britain.

The Romans knew the surveyor as *agrimensor*, literally 'land tabulator'. Writers on the subject were called *gromatici* because the main surveying

A *groma* in use. This instrument consists of four plumb lines; by squinting along them in pairs, a surveyor could establish two lines on the ground that cross at right angles. (*Author's image*)

instrument of the Romans was the *groma*, a square cross set horizontally atop a staff held vertically. Four plummets depended from its extremities. All ancient surveyors probably used this instrument. With its aid, two long lines lying at right angles could be laid out.

The esoteric or philosophical nature of the surveyor is illustrated in a painting entitled *An Allegory of Prophecy* by the Venetian artist Jacopo Palma (Palma Giovane) that hangs in Kingston Lacy House in Dorset. The second most prominent figure, after a king who holds out a book, is one raising aloft a *groma*, wielding it as a staff of intellectual authority, thus proclaiming the king's building achievements – always a preoccupation of authoritarian rulers.

Measuring distances in the ancient world was usually accomplished by pacing. The Greeks had a cadre of men called 'bematists' who counted their steps. Some accompanied Alexander the Great on his campaign in Asia, their task being to determine distances between cities. Their precision was astonishing: over hundreds of miles they could achieve accuracies of 99.6 per cent, as with the distance between Hecatompylos to Alexandria Areion (over

500 miles) although a more typical accuracy was 97–8 per cent (information derived from D. W. Engles, *Alexander the Great and the logistics of the Macedonian army*). Over distances of the order of a Survey Unit it is feasible to employ a chain, or something similar, which must be expected to result in higher precision. If a distance were ritually important, it would have been measured several times to ensure accuracy.

To survey a grid, one first needs to create a set of parallel, equally spaced lines. One line is first established. Then, using the *groma* at a point on the line, a second line is marked out at right angles to it. This line I shall term the baseline. By measuring along this baseline, markers are placed at regular intervals on it. The *groma* is then used at every marker to establish lines at right angles to the baseline. Lines in this latter set will thus be parallel to the original line. The *groma* can be used again at points regularly spaced on the initial line to complete the grid. Imperfections in the arrangement will always exist. There may be small imperfections in the *groma* and limitations to the skill with which it is used. Even with a 'perfect' instrument and a highly skilled operator, truly parallel lines cannot be established over long distances because the surface of the earth is fundamentally spherical, not flat. However, the errors will not be great over the distances considered here.

The most well-known symbolic grid is the Net of Indra (the chief of the Hindu gods) that hangs over Indra's palace. It is infinite in its dimensions, and at every knot Indra placed a perfect jewel, each of which reflects every other jewel. The net is analogous to the whole web of existence: action at one node affects the condition of every other node. The image has naturally become important for Buddhists for whom every element of life is sacred.

We have established that gridding the land was a well-known and well-documented procedure, and have illustrated a simple method of achieving it. We have noted that the intersections of grid lines were marked with stones, in some cases, and can be reasonably sure that in an esoteric grid these stones would achieve an esoteric significance. Grids have many uses; they are familiar to us in the form of graph paper, where one horizontal line is selected as the x-axis and vertical measurements are conducted from it; a vertical line is designated the y-axis from which horizontal measurements are made. Artists contemplating a large work, say a mural, will produce a small version over which they draw a grid, usually a square one; the wall to be decorated is similarly gridded but on a larger scale, and the picture transferred to the wall by positioning its elements with reference to corresponding grid squares on the smaller picture. The reverse procedure is used in making some maps.

Mapping Orion

A similar method was used to construct Orion, but the procedure was aided by the nature of Orion's belt, which consists of three (almost) equally spaced stars lying (almost) in a row. I described the construction of the baseline in the previous chapter. To reiterate: a *groma* was used at Baseline Cottage to strike a line at right angles to the Cosmic Axis. One Survey Unit along this line a marker was created to symbolise the star Mintaka. The marker became the site for a Saxon or Jutish *hearg*, a shrine or temple, naming the place for the future as Harbridge. Subsequently, a Christian church was built at the old pagan site.

One Survey Unit further on and the surveyors could conveniently ignore the fact that the middle star, Al Nilam, was not exactly in the middle and not precisely in line with the outside two – although it may seem so to the casual observer. Given the marshy ground in the flood plain of the Ashford Water, a tributary of the River Avon, no building was erected to mark the place known as Holy Head. However, at a further Survey Unit along the baseline, some kind of marker recorded the position of the analogue of the star Al Nitak, which task is now performed by Martin Church. This simple baseline served to lay out Orion's belt, but this was as much as could be achieved without constructing a grid.

Take the *groma* to each marked point of the baseline, aligning one set of plumb bobs with the line, and sight along the other pair, marking the lines passing through Martin and Harbridge churches and Holy Head. This procedure results in a set of equally spaced lines parallel to the Cosmic Axis. (As noted, the lines cannot be precisely parallel, owing to the curvature of the earth, but the error is small in this case.) Examination of the lines shows that some of the marker sites are also those of ancient churches. The old, but mostly rebuilt, church of St Mary the Virgin at Micheldever falls on a surveyed line, and is a good match for the alpha-star of the constellation, Betelgeuse; it is the only church in the area with the remotest chance of providing a good analogue for the star. (I shall, of course, quantify the differences between the components of the celestial constellation and its terrestrial counterpart and explain the reasons for them.)

A grid needs two sets of complementary lines. The second set has the same spacing as the first and is orientated towards the midsummer's sunset, thus completing a skewed grid. The initial line begins on the massy headland of St Alban's (or St Aldhelm's) Head and passes through the churches of East

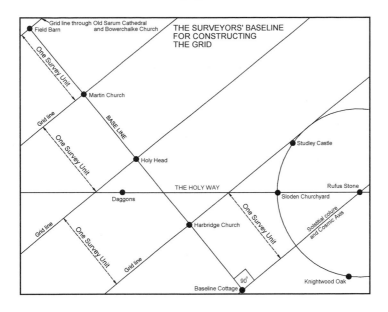

Cokcr, Closworth, Cerne Abbas, Tincleton and Moreton. Tincleton alone is not an ancient church. Moreton Church is the analogue of Orion's left foot, Rigel. A further grid line passes through the church at Buckhorn Weston, the image of Orion's right foot, Saiph. This is as far as the grid could be used for marking out Orion; the position of the faint star Meissa, Orion's eye, does not fit such a convenient model, neither does the prominent star Bellatrix, Orion's left shoulder. Meissa is marked on the ground by the church at Soberton, probably by scaled distance measurement from Micheldever Church at an azimuth calculated from angular measurements of the constellation. Bellatrix is represented by the church at Fawley, and its position is one of supreme interest. Fawley Church appears to have been located as nearly as possible to the sea, without encroaching on marshy ground, and positioned exactly six Survey Units from Micheldever Church. (That is to say, there are points within each church that lie precisely six Survey Units apart.) The precision of this 'across the shoulders' distance is rendered more amazing when it is noted that it crosses two miles of the Southampton Water, and could not have been measured directly by pacing or by using measuring rods. The easy way to explain this accuracy is to put it down to chance; but not only is it a slim chance to discover a distance measured in integral multiples of Survey Units in a figure determined largely by a grid based on Survey Units, it is a fact that Micheldever Church – Betelgeuse – lies exactly six Survey Units from the

Rufus Stone. Discovering the answers to the questions of how the surveyors accomplished precision measurement across water, and why, is fascinating, but will have to await a church-by-church examination of the terrestrial Orion.

The churches of Orion

On the basis of place-name evidence, Harbridge Church, rebuilt in about 1835, dedicated to All Saints, and the analogue of the star Mintaka, was originally built on or near the site of a *hearg*, as we have noted. So often were Christian churches erected on pagan sites that Pope Gregory had to formalise the practice. In a permissive letter of AD 601 to Abbot Mellitus he instructed Augustine, who was then on a mission to the pagan English, to preserve pagan temples, purifying them with holy water, and replacing their idols with saintly relics. Much the same accommodation with the peasantry was made by the Roman Catholic Church in South America, where many 'Christian' festivals contain obviously pre-Christian ritual routines and symbols. Gregory was aware that a place marked as special in the popular imagination could not be destroyed, for it is part of the fabric of the earth. One cannot ignore it either; otherwise its old spirits would remain unexpurgated. One can only colonise it, exploit its resources, and deny it as a redoubt to one's enemies. The building of a Christian cathedral within the spectacular mosque of Mezquita in Cordoba was an act of vandalism justified by such politics.

Holy Head, conveniently imprecisely marked, represents the star Al Nilam ('the string of pearls') but has no church. Martin Church, also dedicated to All Saints, is unremarkable and represents the star Al Nitak ('the girdle'). It contains Norman work, but most of the fabric is of later date. These three locations together make up 'Orion's belt', a star grouping that possessed a mythological meaning independent of the constellation of Orion in some cultures. The names of the several stars were all applied indiscriminately to the belt and were only gradually awarded to its individual members.

Saiph, the right foot of Orion, is a name derived from the same root as the Greek *sophos*, meaning 'complex wisdom'. Buckhorn Weston, which is its analogue, is dedicated to St John the Baptist. In an easily understandable sense, Orion stands upon the wisdom of the Johannites, among whom are numbered the Knights Templar and modern Freemasons.

Moreton Church

Moreton Church is the analogue of the star Rigel, Orion's left foot. It stands on the right bank of the River Frome (the Lesser Frome, that is). It is ancient but has been rebuilt. It was originally dedicated to St Magnus of Orkney, a seemingly strange dedication for a church in south Dorset; but Magnus, as his name implies, was a large man. Orion of Wessex is a large man, too, so the dedication is more apt than may be immediately apparent. The church was then dedicated to St Nicholas, the patron saint of sailors, and this is also apt, for Rigel had marine connections: the third-century saint, St Marinus, is said to have owed his festal day, 3 March, to the rising of Rigel. Currently, Magnus and Nicholas share the dedication.

German aircraft bombed the church on the night of 8 October 1940. It is thought that the bombing was accidental, the aircraft aiming to hit Bovington Camp using a novel form of navigation; the idea was to fly along a single radio beam (unlike the British Oboe method of intersecting beams) employing some form of distance measurement to locate the target. Moreton Church suffered structural damage and lost all its windows. They have been replaced by a wonderful set of etched clear-glass lights by the artist Laurence Whistler. These windows ensure that Moreton Church is one of the lightest old churches in the country. Although Rigel is Orion's beta star (the second-ranking star in the constellation, Betelgeuse being the alpha star) Rigel is now the brightest one. How appropriate to find the brightest star of Orion matching what must be the brightest church in its terrestrial equivalent!

Whistler used local features in some of the pictures; in the vestry window, a lightning flash forms a map of the River Frome, by which the church stands, its position marked by a circle of ball lightning – representing, too, the German bomb that damaged it. The window bears the biblical quotation, 'He maketh lightning'. Whistler has defined a sacred, symbolic landscape by means of this image: God created lightning, therefore God created the river and the church. This part of the landscape is thus endowed with a sacred mantle. A clever theological point is also encoded in the image. The source of the Frome lies in St John's Well, Evershot. The river can therefore be seen as an analogue of the River Jordan, in which John the Baptist performed his baptisms. The gospels imply a valid but subsidiary function for St John as an originator of the Christian faith. Echoing this theology, the river begins with him, widens as it flows, and comes to full power when it reaches the church at Moreton. The artist has provided us with another clue to spatial order: in Chapter 8 we

Above: Moreton Church. (*Author's image, reproduced by permission of the Rector*)

Left: A window from Moreton Church by Laurence Whistler showing the River Frome as a lightning stroke and Moreton Church as ball lightning. (*Author's image, reproduced by permission of the Rector*)

shall discover that Whistler was not the first to regard the River Frome as a sacred watercourse. In fact, we shall be left wondering whether our discovery was not the source of Whistler's imagination.

Our attention should now turn to Betelgeuse, whose name means 'armpit of the giant'. My reference to it as 'a shoulder' is thus not too anatomically remote. We should expect great importance to attach to the alpha star of the constellation: Micheldever Church ought to display impressive symbols of power.

Micheldever Church

John Baring left his native Bremen in the early 1700s and set up as a cloth manufacturer near Exeter. His son Francis (1740–1810) became the leading merchant in Europe and amassed seven million pounds before he died – immense wealth for the period. This Francis was knighted, and it was he who founded Barings Bank. His son Alexander was elevated to the peerage, becoming the 1st Baron Ashburton.

Micheldever was a royal vill in AD 862. King Alfred willed it to the New Minster of Winchester. It came into the possession of the Dukes of Bedford who sold it to Sir Francis Baring in 1801. In 1805, the fabric of the ancient church at Micheldever was deemed unsafe and pulled down, although its tower was sound and remains intact. (Legend has it, and it is reported as fact in some accounts – but is contrary to the historical version – that the old church at Micheldever was not deliberately pulled down in 1805, but was accidentally burned.) Sir Francis Baring rebuilt the nave and chancel to a design of the architect George Dance the Younger. Later, the architect Coulson made modifications. Beautiful Baring memorials by the noted sculptor John Flaxman flank and dominate the walls of the chancel. The nave was reconstructed as an octagon, which is the basis of the Maltese cross, the emblem of the Knights of St John. The ceiling is decorated with stars.

When Pope Clement V forcibly disbanded the hugely rich and influential order of the Knights Templar in 1312, some of its members found safe haven in Scotland. There, later, their secrets and ceremonies became incorporated in advanced levels of Freemasonry from where they have spread more widely. The Templars are recorded as having charge of his regalia and the ordering of affairs when King John gave his assent to Magna Carta at Runnymede. The Earl Marshall – a post filled from 1672 by the Dukes of Norfolk who, in this capacity, arrange the details of coronations – has since performed these functions. The Dukes become members of the present Order of St John. The change in responsibility from the Templars to the Earls Marshall (originally simply 'Marshall') occurred in the reign of Edward II. He clearly received astrological advice after that date for he fought the disastrous (for the English) Battle of Bannockburn on Midsummer's Day, 1314. The incompetence, or malice, of his astrologer was repeated: Edward's barbarous murder was arranged for the autumnal equinox in 1327. Edward had a taste for things chivalric and ceremonial, a taste inherited and cultivated by his son Edward III, who turned his court into a veritable Camelot.

The former prerogatives and responsibilities of the Templars lost their dourness in the hands of their new custodians. Chivalry blossomed throughout Europe. But this was the vernacular face of tradition. Ancient rites and ceremonies still had to be observed, for it was the application of ancient formulae that conferred legitimacy. Nowhere was this more important than in coronation ceremonies. Edward II had been crowned sitting over the Stone of Destiny, or Stone of Scone, brought to Westminster in 1297 from Scone Abbey, where the kings of Scotland had been crowned. It was stolen (or retrieved, according to one's opinion) and secretly removed to Arbroath Abbey by Scottish nationalists in 1950. The thirteenth-century romance *Parzival* confirms a link between the Knights Templar and a legendary Stone of Destiny; it makes them its guardians. After four months of tremendous effort, the police recovered the Stone, which has since been returned officially to Scotland. The fear in 1950 was that any monarch not crowned on it would lack the legitimate right, preserved by custom, to reign. Any concern for the detail of ritual that applies today would have been doubly important in medieval times when constitutional stability was weaker than it is now. We can be sure, therefore, that ritual lore did not die with the Templars, but has been conveyed down to present times. Obviously, Sir Francis Baring obtained his knowledge of the symbolic importance of Micheldever from somewhere. The style of his rebuilding works strongly suggests that it is the Templar connection, possibly transmitted through Freemasonry and its associated societies, that supplied his information.

Fawley Church

Banking was not a profession confined to the Baring family, of course. The gentry at Fawley, whose church is the analogue of Bellatrix, were also bankers. The Honourable Robert Drummond, third son of Viscount Strathallan, was

An engraving of Fawley Church from Robert Mudie's *Hampshire, its past and present condition, and future prospects*, 1840.

sent to London to work in his uncle's banking company to avoid the political unrest then being fomented in Scotland. The Viscount was killed fighting for the Jacobite cause at the Battle of Culloden in 1746, but Robert became a governor of the bank and bought, in 1772, the Manor of Cadland in the parish of Fawley, where he built a fine Palladian house. The Drummonds married into the nobility, and even once entertained King George III at Fawley. The king bore no grudge against the family for their Jacobite connection. (He had even paid for the memorial to Bonnie Prince Charlie in Rome.)

The Drummond family has no sculpted memorials in Fawley Church; past members of the family are commemorated by a series of brass plates set within a stone arcade under the tower. However, as an aristocratic Jacobite, Viscount Strathallan would have certainly been a Freemason, and his sons probably followed him in that tradition. It is known that a family member, George Drummond, Lord Provost of Edinburgh, was Grand Master of Scottish Freemasonry in 1752. We can be sure that whatever esoteric lore pertains to the relative siting of the churches at Micheldever and Fawley, the Baring and the Drummond families shared it. Bankers they both were to successive sovereigns, but banking in Europe originated with the Templars, who also acted as bankers and financial advisers to their kings. Some Templars escaped the pogrom of

Philip IV of France and Pope Clement V who violently attacked the order in 1307 and plundered its assets. The survivors raised families who continued the tradition and profession of banking. By marriage and inheritance, an unbroken line of banking families was established reaching back from the present to the twelfth century. Old 'Templar' families sometimes adopted the five-pointed star (the mullet) in their coats of arms, as the Barings did with their crest.

While Fawley Church's mural monuments cannot help us, the floor is not without an interesting memorial. Close to the wall in the south chapel lies the 'Crusader's grave', moved from a site between two nearby pillars in 1990. This is no fancy monument with a recumbent, cross-legged knight, but a plain stone slab without inscription. A long Calvary cross is sculpted on the slab, above which are carved four trefoils in a circular arrangement. The memorial is absolutely characteristic of a tomb of a Knight Templar. It is without parallel in the churches of the area. Micheldever Church has its rare but relatively recent Templar-pattern nave, while Fawley Church can boast its own rare and ancient Templar grave. We can never know if the individual once buried beneath the slab was a high dignitary of the Knights of the Temple of Solomon or whether his was the role of 'the unknown warrior'. There is no clear reason why he should be there, unless it was as a 'ritual deposit'; in which case the warrior is superbly

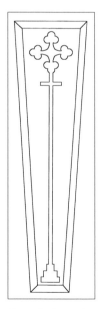

Crusader's tomb slab in Fawley Church.

fitted for placement in one of the 'pits' marking out the constellation of Orion. The two shoulders of Orion are thus seen to have strong connections with the Knights Templar, through the banking profession, and the architectural and memorial aspects of their respective churches.

The image of the dedicated knight with drawn sword is one to inspire feelings of confidence that right will prevail. It is the masculine equivalent of the lady with the drawn sword holding the scales of Justice. The Knight Templar in this context is also Bellatrix made man. He was sworn to chastity, thus renouncing his male attribute. In so doing he became an androgynous (or neutral) symbol for all humans, just as Joan of Arc, 'the Maid', symbolised the whole French nation in its conflict with the English. Fawley's position at the edge of the land suggests that the knight or maiden warrior is defending England's shores against its foes. I shall now explore the liminal aspects of Orion suggested by a littoral position, and leave further considerations of Justice to the next chapter.

Liminal considerations

Liminality has already entered our story. It is apparent in the coastal properties of Flowers Barrow and Lowestoft Ness, reinforced by their respective 'highest' and 'furthest east' characteristics of points defining an axis. It occurs, too, with Baggy Point and St Margaret at Cliffe, both coastal positions defining a line with a 'longest' attribute. More generally, liminality in literature and philosophy is the mystical properties of thresholds and boundaries, both physical and metaphorical ones, of 'in-between' situations and entities, of psychic enclaves. Liminal landscape elements include the effectively infinite ones of shoreline and riverbank, and discrete components like caves, isolated hills, steps and enclosures. Lakes with islands are supremely liminal, and figure strongly in mystical literature and verse. In a process of accelerating liminality, one enters the churchyard, then the porch, next passing through the church door, finally proceeding from nave to chancel to pause at the communion rail, which marks the boundary of a privileged area containing the altar where the ultimate ritual of the Eucharist is performed. This creation of thresholds and linked enclaves not only conditions the experience of the individual worshipper but gives meaning to corporate processions through them; specific acts of both static and dynamic religious observance are thereby enabled. This example is situated in the horizontal plane, a space accessible to mortals: Sebald's shrine is liminally stratified in the vertical plane, through which only souls, spirits and angels, never subordinate to the laws of gravity, can traverse.

Liminality is illustrated in the tenth chapter of the Book of Revelation, where the seventh angel is described as standing with one foot in the sea and the other on dry land. Moreton Church lies on the bank of the River Frome, Harbridge Church on the bank of the River Avon, and Fawley Church on the

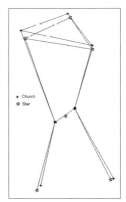

A comparison of the constellation of Orion and its image on the ground. In this case the stars of the belt have been made to coincide with the churches representing them.

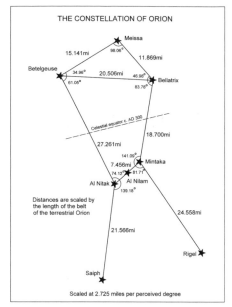

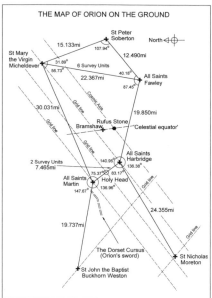

edge of the Southampton Water. Orion's left side is washed by water in contrast to his right side, all of whose elements are well inland and firmly on dry land. Liminal Orion stands guardian between the dwellers of the land and the evil spirits and material dangers of the waters. Liminality is also concerned with intermediates; Holy Head, the middle star of the belt, lies on the flood plain of the Ashford Water, a place dry and water-covered by turn, neither wholly one realm nor the other, and in this case geographically central between the waters and the land as represented by Harbridge and Martin churches respectively. Orion holds within himself this magical, spiritual or 'holy' territory. All caves, crypts and catacombs, natural or artificial, lie below ground yet are not part of the earth, supposed dwellings of spirits, either of the dead or of those never mortal, to be visited by pilgrims seeking knowledge, guidance, favours, or absolution. The earthwork enclosures of Sloden Churchyard and Studley Castle are both liminal because they stand symbolically at the edge of the known world as modelled by the circle centred on the Rufus Stone.

It would appear that the four most important determinants of symbolic sites are liminality, anthropomorphic characteristics, centrality and celestial equivalence. The Cosmic Axis and the Wessex Orion posses all these qualities in good measure, but they form only part of a grander heavenly pattern with extensive liminal properties.

7

ORION: HUNTER, SHEPHERD, JUDGE

Forget it not, when Orion first appears
To make your servants thresh the sacred ears.

Hesiod (*Works and Days*)

Who is Orion?

Orion was the most important constellation for the ancient Egyptians, and interpreted by them as representative of Osiris, the god of the underworld. But he had many other identities, probably even among the ancient Egyptians, which is not surprising regarding his spectacular appearance and anthropomorphic configuration, both of which ensure his identification with heroes across ages and cultures.

For the Greeks and the Romans, Orion's birth was unusual, even by mythological standards. The three gods Jupiter, Neptune and Mercury, as they travelled through Boeotia (a region of ancient Greece), met with great hospitality from Hyricus, a peasant who was at first ignorant of their dignity and character. He entertained them with the little he had. When he discovered their identities, he sacrificed an ox for their pleasure. Well pleased, the gods undertook to grant him one wish. Hyricus had no son, and being a widower who had vowed never to remarry, he asked the gods for one. They all then urinated into the hide of the ox, which they ordered Hyricus to bury in the ground. Nine months later he dug it up, finding within it a beautiful boy child whom he named Urion after the holy urine from which he had sprung. The Roman poet Ovid claimed that the more familiar spelling is a corruption.

The father of the gods, Zeus, sired Artemis, goddess of the moon and a huntress, also known as Diana or Phoebe. Artemis fell in love with Orion, but he became enamoured of a group of nymphs, whom he pursued. Artemis saved them from Orion's attentions by turning them into a flock of white doves; they can be seen as the stars in the constellation of the Pleiades. Orion then fell in love with a princess named Merope. His only hope of marrying her was by abduction, but her father, Oenopion, frustrated Orion's plan by intoxicating him, making him lie down next to the sea, and blinding him. (This part of Orion's legend may account for the terrestrial Orion's disposition near the coasts of Hampshire and Dorset.) Orion stumbled aimlessly about the forest, eventually reaching the cave of the Cyclopes, a race of one-eyed giants, one of whom brought him to a place where the rising sun was seen to greatest advantage and where his sight was restored. (Some claim that a blacksmith performed this service.) Orion and Artemis resumed their friendship, but Apollo, the twin brother of Artemis, became jealous. He called Artemis to his side and sought to test her skill in archery by asking her to shoot at a speck rising from the sea. Artemis was unaware that the speck was Orion's head. She mourned his death and placed him in the heavens with his faithful hound Sirius.

For the ancient Jews, Orion was Nimrod, the mighty hunter. To the Babylonians, the constellation represented Tammuz, the equivalent of the Greek Adonis (literally, 'Lord'). The meaning of Tammuz's name is 'true son of the deep water'. He was the lover of the mother goddess Ishtar. Every year he died and rose again, just as Orion disappears from the northern skies in summer to reappear as winter returns. The Babylonians' name for Orion meant 'faithful shepherd'. Sirius, the brightest star, dogging Orion's heels, was his sheepdog. This image became known as the Good Shepherd, which was adopted as a title by the kings of the Egypt and Mesopotamia over two millennia before the Christian era. Jesus, the ultimate icon of guardianship, also adopted it, as reported in St John's Gospel. For its first two hundred years, the Christian Church lacked a comprehensive symbolism of its own, but it borrowed the image of the Good Shepherd and used it in its catacombs, rendered as a man carrying a sheep in his arms or bearing it on his shoulders.

Turning to Germano-Scandinavian mythology we find Orion as Odin, chief of the Nordic gods, who sought wisdom from an old man named Mimir, a name meaning 'memory', who guarded a magic fountain. Mimir's price for the wisdom and wit conferred by a draught from his fountain was one of Odin's eyes, a price that Odin readily paid. To celebrate his newfound wisdom,

Odin plucked a branch from the Tree of Life, Yggdrasil, and from it fashioned a spear, Gungnir. He hung nine days and nights on Yggdrasil and wounded himself with his spear to gain the knowledge of writing. Afterwards, he carved runic inscriptions on Gungnir. Odin is best known as a wanderer, bearing his spear and followed by his two dogs. As with Orion, one dog is certainly Sirius, the brightest star; the other is probably Procyon, the alpha star of the constellation Canis Minor, the Small Dog. There are strong correspondences with Greek and Roman stories of Orion, the sacrifice of an eye in exchange for wisdom, for example. Odin's hanging on the Tree of Life again mirrors what is found in the Wessex countryside.

Was Orion the Sumerian Gilgamesh, the oldest heroic figure in literature? The story of Gilgamesh was found in the excavated library of the great Syrian king Ashurbanipal who ruled in the seventh century BC, although other texts have since been discovered. It is thought to be far older than this date, surviving for centuries in an oral form. Gilgamesh was born from the union of a goddess and a man during a New Year festival. He, and a wild man named Enkidu, created by the mother goddess Aruru from clay wetted with spittle, killed a fire-breathing giant named Humbaba with the aid of the sun god Shamash. At one point in the story, Gilgamesh fells a magic tree and fashions a drum and a drumstick from it. The drumstick he lets fall into the nether regions. The parallels between the drumstick and its fate, and Odin's Gungnir and the orientation of Orion's 'shaft' towards the winter sunrise, are striking.

An obvious candidate for Orion is Mithras, for he fought the bull: the pattern of constellations fixed by the ancients shows Orion squaring up to Taurus, but some scholars prefer to equate him with the constellation of Perseus. Orion could be an icon of their master for disciples of John the Baptist: Meissa, the only indication of Orion's head, is a very weak star so the constellation is perfect for representing a decapitated body.

St Michael the Archangel is a powerful figure in the Hebrew, Christian and Islamic traditions; his equivalent in ancient Greece was the messenger of the gods, Hermes, who also conducted the souls of the departed to heaven and guarded secret – hermetic – knowledge. St Michael's name means 'he who resembles god', so his representation by Orion must be considered too. The emblem of Hermes is the caduceus, a rod about which twine two serpents; some illustrations of it include two wings at the top, and sometimes a winged dragon. It is difficult to avoid the conclusion that the caduceus is the Cosmic Axis, specifically in its guise as the Tree of Life. The serpents are emblems of knowledge and their spiral configuration suggests rotation of the rod. The serpents appeared on the primeval mound in some of the Egyptian creation myths. The presence of a dragon at the top of the rod, and its suggested rotation, confirm the rod as the solstitial colure passing through the north ecliptic pole, which is located in the constellation of Draco. Here, we may have a four-thousand-year-old folk memory of the time before precession nudged the pole star Thuban and the rest of Draco away from the summit of creation, just as it moved – and is moving – the sun away from the signs of the Zodiac to which it was originally assigned throughout the year.

Did the astral figure of Orion the hunter give rise to the legend of St Michael slaying the dragon of winter with the rotating golden solstitial shaft? We read in the Book of Revelation (12:7-8) how there was war in heaven, and how Michael and his angels fought the dragon, overcoming him. The popular icon of the Archangel Michael, the one depicted in art, is of an armoured knight thrusting his sword, spear or lance into a writhing dragon. Painted and sculpted images of the slaying of the dragon abound. But St Michael has another ritual function: it is he who weighs the souls of the dead to assess whether they deserve to enter heaven. Christian images of St Michael exist showing him bearing the scales of justice. The Greeks have a tradition that only the dead or those about to die can see the face of St Michael, which accords with the constellation of Orion possessing no head, only the faint and much ignored eye, the star Meissa. The likeness of blindfolded Justice outside our law courts not only signifies that Justice is blind to the identity of the accused, but that she, too, cannot be recognised as an individual. Likewise, when Justice has done her work, the headsman is masked so that the felon cannot associate his executioner with an individual: the state is the dispassionate and impersonal executioner. The association of the left side of the terrestrial Orion with water, as we have seen, is in keeping with the Kabbalah's association of St Michael with the 'element' water. In the Book of Enoch (24; 25) St Michael is portrayed as the Guardian of the Heavenly Jerusalem and of the Tree of Life, as fits the configuration in the Wessex countryside.

Without distorting the image of the heavenly pattern too much, the right leg of the terrestrial Orion could be extended so that he 'stands' in South Cadbury Castle, an Iron Age earthwork, which is unaccountably known locally as Camelot. So is Orion King Arthur? Arthur owned the magical sword Excalibur, which means 'from the measurer'. Was Merlin, from whom he obtained the sword, a personification of the Measurer, Thoth, and what did it measure and how? Not only the sword but its scabbard, too, was magical. 'Excalibur' could mean, alternatively, the sword 'drawn from the calibrating device'. Was the scabbard the measure of a Survey Unit or a Celestial Unit? Remarkably, in plan, the Dorset Cursus seems to hang from the belt of the Wessex Orion – a perfect scabbard. But this is the image in the skies, too, for the beautiful Orion Nebula, a misty collection of stars and stellar dust, seems to hang from the celestial belt. It is the brightest nebula in the heavens; stars in it were noted in Ptolomy's catalogue of AD 130, and an early Latin name for it was Ensis, 'the Sword'. If the scabbard is a unit of measurement, it is one by which to measure the sky, for the Dorset Cursus measures a Celestial Unit overall. Perhaps elements of the Arthur/Merlin story do reach back to an earlier age when a sword-bearing solar hero was created by a Thoth figure. But if so, they serve to mark the persistence of a dramatic theme set in a British national context; while of absorbing interest, they are 'secondary reference material' and unlikely to assist us here.

This review of Orion's characterisations could be greatly extended, but sufficient evidence has been presented to show the universal nature of the being associated with the constellation. He is usually powerful and wise, connected with the sun god, often a bearer of a shaft or spear. What is striking is that, apart from the Babylonian Tammuz, perhaps, none of them can be thought of as resembling Osiris, except for some common instances of a single eye. There is a certain degree of universality, but a wide spectrum of characteristics too. Two important points emerge from this assessment: first, we should not be constrained by any one cultural image when attempting to identify the god behind the Wessex Orion; secondly, he may possess multiple personalities or fulfil several roles.

How to create a universe

There is no help for it; to appreciate what follows, the reader will have temporarily to abandon his hard-won philosophical outlook and become attuned to thinking like a Wessex Pythagorean.

The multiplicity of creation myths demonstrates mankind's intense and universal preoccupation with the question of how we, and everything around us, came to be here at all. One way to explain existence is to credit 'god' with creating it, which inevitably raises the question of who created god. For many, the answer is avoidance: 'god was always there'. It is the same with the Big Bang theory: 'time has no meaning before the Big Bang'. Both these differing perceptions, of infinite time and of no time, are counter-intuitive, although one of them is possibly correct. More satisfying is the ancient Egyptians' recursive answer that 'god created himself'; time is thereby wrapped up into an infinitesimal ball where it has an existence but is invisible.

In exactly the same way that the Big Bang starts with a point, so Egyptian and Pythagorean creation began with a point: the emergence of the primordial mound in the primeval ocean. Inflation and expansion amplified the point of the Big Bang to the space that now defines the known universe. The Pythagoreans created space in a different way: they progressively expanded the number of its dimensions to provide a home for humans, stars, and all else. First came the *point* represented by the mound. Then came the *line*, the Cosmic Axis, defined by the sun, imparting an additional dimension to existence. The theological reasoning seems to be that with the emergence of the mound, light was automatically separated from darkness, and that particular phenomenon required the presence of the sun; the sun was an implicit consequence of the initial act of emergence, and not a product of subsequent creation. But the sun was regarded as only the *symbol* of a god; a 'real' god was urgently needed to create the rest of the universe, the other dimensions. And it is here that the Pythagorean contention that number is the basis of the universe comes into play. For them, number was not attached to time; it had an independent existence. Wherever you were in the universe, at whatever time, you would be able to discover the same mathematics; it was a universal philosophy, free (in theory) from the subjectivity of mythology. What I have called Wessex Vitruvian Man, a personification of the creator god who was not created by any other agency, was *defined* by number, by the proportions of the human (and hence divine) body, according to the Fibonacci series, the natural, mathematical process of increase. The concept became the reality. But this was still not yet a fully dimensioned space in which creation could continue. Vitruvian Man needed to recreate himself with an extra dimension as a *planar* image. How did he achieve that?

The Egyptian myths are clear about the process: the god ejaculated a stream of semen that seeded the rest of creation. More specifically, 'our' Thoth produced a germinal 'string of pearls', now represented in Wessex by Harbridge Church, Holy Head and Martin Church. From these precious, viable drops creating Orion's Belt sprang the rest of the fully dimensioned god, again by the application of measurement – the use of number. Thoth now had enough self-generated dimensions to perform his multitude of other tasks.

It is the task of weighing souls in a balance to determine their further course that confirms the Wessex Orion as being an image of Thoth, for his scales will be discovered.

Law for the many, Justice for the few

In a spectacular and easily comprehensible way, according to established philosophies, the Wessex landscape displays a pictorial representation of the Creation as imagined by an intelligent and knowledgeable school of philosophers intellectually suspended between myth-based religion and scientific rationalism. But mankind's interest in his origins is heavily outweighed by his preoccupation with where he is going next. Heaven or Hell? Everlasting life or eternal damnation? Thoth – and his Christian understudy, St Michael – decided the vital issue with a pair of scales. Thoth weighed the heart against a feather, the weight of which was the greatest allowable burden of unatoned sin. What St Michael weighed is unclear, but some fifteenth-century European paintings depict him as weighing one human-looking soul against another.

The Scales – Libra – is a constellation lying on the ecliptic, and is hence a sign of the Zodiac. It consists of a small, insignificant triangle of stars (with instantly forgettable names) comprising the beam and includes other stars meant to portray the dangling scale pans. A clue to findings Thoth's Libra is contained in an early fifteenth-century icon in Archangel Cathedral in the Kremlin, which shows a triangular belt stretched across the hips of St Michael; Libra has been represented by the obvious triangle of the balance beam. However, in Wessex it is not Orion's belt that forms Libra; Justice demands that the scale beam is perfect, and for the Pythagoreans this meant that it had to be exactly six Survey Units in length because for them six was the first perfect number. (Recall that 6 = 1 + 2 + 3, the sum of its divisors.) This is the distance between Micheldever Church and Fawley Church. These two churches, together with Soberton Church, form a triangle with proportions very close to the triangle of the constellation of Libra. The terrestrial Orion, alias Thoth, alias St Michael, bears the scales of Justice on his shoulders, and his otherwise invisible face comes into view as that of Justice by those who are about to undergo the weighing of their souls.

Surveying the beam

Readers who find all references to mathematics irritating can skip the rest of this chapter, but they need to accept that there is indeed a simple method to site two churches exactly six Survey Units apart without making a direct traverse from one to the other.

The problem is, having determined the site of Micheldever Church, to establish the location at which to build Fawley Church when the line crosses the Southampton Water. The simplest (and hence potentially the most accurate) method would be to lay out two sides of a triangle over land such that the third side would connect Micheldever and Fawley. For convenience, let's call the apex of this triangle point A. There exist several constraints on the properties of the triangle. First, for accuracy's sake, the sides should be of comparable length; secondly, it should not cross the valley of the River Avon, for this would compound the difficulties of measurement; thirdly, for ease of computation, it should contain a right angle. An advantage would also exist if the right angle were made to occur at Fawley, for then, if the inevitable spot were unsuitable for a building, simple adjustments in its position could be made to maintain the length of the line at six Survey Units; another advantage is that the right angle at Fawley would minimise the error in measuring the beam consequent upon a given error in measuring the line from point A to Fawley. We should expect point A to be a site of some note, possibly possessing a connection with justice, or at least the law.

When a triangle contains a right angle, it is possible to exploit the theorem of Pythagoras, which states (effectively) that the length of the hypotenuse (the side opposite the right angle) is equal to the square root of the sum of the squares of the lengths of the other two sides. Given that one side of the triangle is required to be six Survey Units in length, it would be computationally and cartographically sensible (as will emerge) and symbolically attractive to make the other side bordering the right angle also an integral number of Survey Units in length.

The surveyors also used a property of similar triangles. If a particular triangle is enlarged (or reduced) by projection, its angles remain unchanged, provided that the ratios of the three sides are unaltered, as is usually the case with projection. All such triangles so produced are called 'similar'.

With all these points in mind, let's look at the map and work backwards. Draw the line from Micheldever to Fawley and strike a line at right angles to it through Fawley (roughly, just north of west). Six Survey Units would take us across the River Avon, which is undesirable, but five Survey Units lands us well on the eastern bank of the river. In fact, we arrive at Moyles Court.

Moyles Court, now a Restoration mansion, is recorded in 1398 as being in the hands of the Moeles family. It possesses the required association with justice, for baronial courts were held there. It is best known as the home of Dame Alice Lisle, who was condemned to death in 1685 by the infamous Judge

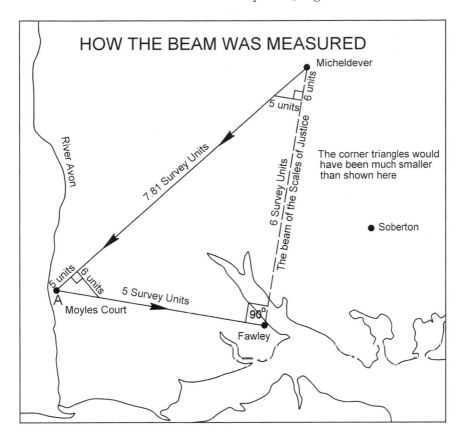

Jeffreys for harbouring two fugitives from the failed Monmouth rebellion. Alice's late husband, John, had drafted the warrant for the beheading of Charles I, and Oliver Cromwell had made him Keeper of the Great Seal of the Commonwealth. There was ample reason for the restored monarchy to seek revenge on the Lisle family. Dame Alice's confrontation with her arresters is depicted as a mural in the Houses of Parliament, thus Moyles Court finds reference within England's supreme court of law: curious.

So how was the survey conducted? A sighting rod was erected at a point over which would later be built Micheldever Church, and the direction of the beam (the angle determined from the heavenly constellation) was marked out as a short line from it, that is, pointing towards Fawley. A point six units long was marked along this line from its beginning. For the sake of illustration, I shall consider a unit ten yards in length, but any convenient unit would have sufficed. Our point thus lies sixty yards along the line. From this point, using a *groma* or a 3:4:5 triangle (which contains a right angle), a line was marked out on the ground, five units (fifty yards in my illustration) in length; another sighting rod was erected at this point. Sighting along the two rods, further rods were progressively erected in the standard line-surveying manner, continuing towards point A. The length of this line called for careful measurement. Using Pythagoras' theorem, the distance needed to be travelled could be calculated; it is the square root of six squared plus five squared, which sum is 61. The advantage of using integral multiples of a unit is now apparent, for it is a simple procedure to calculate the square root of 61; a very good initial approximation could be found by measuring the hypotenuse of the small triangle created initially (or any similar triangle) and improved upon by trial and error calculations. In practice, the value of 7.81 Survey Units was an accurate enough distance to measure between Micheldever and point A (7.81 × 7.81 = 60.9961, close enough to 61). The value of 78.1 yards for its hypotenuse could have been used to verify that the small triangle (with sides 60 yards and 50 yards in my illustration) did indeed include a right angle. Point A, now identified as Moyles Court, was established and a sighting rod erected there. The surveyors backtracked along the line five units (50 yards, say) and from there struck a line at right angles, roughly towards the southeast, six units (60 yards, say) in length at the end of which they erected another sighting rod. Sighting on this rod from point A, they measured out a distance of five Survey Units. Having done this they had reached what is now the site of Fawley Church, and the beam of the scales of justice was exactly, it was hoped, six Survey Units in length. Of course, the procedure would have been subject to many checks, and repeated several times, to ensure accuracy. The precision was eventually achieved to within the dimensions of a normally sized church: a great achievement.

Having dispensed with this essential point, we shall now move further into Wessex, and establish Orion's place in our simulated universe.

8

THE MILKY WAY, THE GOLDEN RIVER OF DORSET, AND PARADISE

Standing alone are the ill-fated remains of the River Eridanus, River of Many Tears … winding its way from beneath Orion's left foot…

Aratus of Soli (*Heavenly Phenomena*)

The fisher priest

The Wessex Orion has two other functions to perform, which are both interesting in their own right but confirm his existence as a deliberately created image of the constellation. I shall draw on two different mythological themes inspired by Orion's image and his proximity to the Milky Way in the sky. For both of these, I need to identify the longest east–west line in the country, from Baggy Point in the west to St Margaret's at Cliffe in the east, as an analogue of the Milky Way. This is the line upon which the eighteenth-century eccentric William Benson re-erected a medieval gatehouse as the axial terminus of his Palladian villa.

For those unfamiliar with the Milky Way, it is observable as a ragged band of faint light that circles the heavens, formed from the shining of innumerable and immensely distant stars that belong to the thin disc of matter constituting our own galaxy, which we obviously observe nearly edge-on, because we lie within it, and whose name we confer by analogy. The great circle of best fit to the Milky Way is called the Galactic Equator, and it cuts the Celestial Equator at an angle of about sixty-two degrees. Being composed of 'fixed stars', the Galactic Equator does not change its position over time in relation to the other fixed stars familiar to us as the constituents of the much nearer – relatively – constellations of our galaxy.

I need to refer to the myth of the fish and the ring. The story occurs in one form or another in folk tales around the world. It is old as well as widespread, for it was related by Prince Baufre, son of King Cheops, builder of the Great Pyramid. Baufre tells how Zazamonkh, the chief magician to King Sneferu, retrieved, by parting the waters, the malachite fish pendant belonging to a maiden whom Sneferu took boating on the palace lake. One later version tells how a lady of humble birth, 'never before kissed', married a lord. Her wicked father-in-law cast her wedding ring into the sea and she was expelled from home because she could not produce the token of her marriage. While working in the kitchens of her husband's castle, she finds the ring inside a fish delivered to her by a mysterious fisherman and is thus able to regain her rightful status.

So loaded with symbolic importance is this tale that it found its way into the New Testament. Chapter 17 of St Matthew's Gospel gives the Christian version of the legend. Peter and Jesus are in Capernaum when Peter is asked by the priests to pay the local temple tax. The pair do not carry money (a custom observed by British royalty until recent times) so Jesus tells Peter, the fisherman, to cast his line into the Sea of Galilee and open the first fish that he catches, for inside would be the required four-drachma piece (the most famous example, and the one most probably in the mind of the gospel mythographer, being that minted at Cnossus in the first century BC, which depicted Apollo on its obverse and the Minoan labyrinth on its reverse). The story has been responsible for the halibut ('holy plaice') becoming known as 'St Peter's fish', for it displays a spot on either side of its head – the fingerprints – where Peter grasped it.

St Kentigern, the Pictish patron saint of Glasgow, recovered the wedding ring belonging to a queen from the mouth of a salmon that he sent to find it. It had dropped into the water when she removed it from her finger so that she could commit an act of adultery without sin. Kentigern's action enabled her to regain her position and her virtue. The story is depicted in both the former and the present coats of arms of the City of Glasgow.

Despite its antiquity and its widespread occurrence, most authoritative reference books on folklore ignore the story; those that don't treat it with brevity. Sometimes a pearl is described instead of a ring or coin, and this object is usually associated with wisdom; the salmon that retrieves it represents knowledge. Whatever the meaning of the legend, it seems to be the 'roundness' and 'precious' properties of the lost/found object that are important. The fisherman – the holy man – cannot recover the round object himself but needs the agency of a fish that he can petition, catch, or control.

Former Arms of the City of Glasgow, from *The book of public arms* by A. C. Fox-Davies and M. B. E. Crookes, 1894. (*Reproduced after consultation with Glasgow City Council*)

Glastonbury

Glastonbury is a godsend for those disposed to construct or reinforce their beliefs by means of myth and legend instead of reason and experience. Little remains there apart from the ruins of the grand medieval church of St Peter and St Paul, yet it is generally regarded as the most holy Christian site in England, and the Church of England mounts pilgrimages to its grassy, stone-strewn swards every midsummer. Some claim that the earliest Christian church above ground, a wattle construction dedicated to the mother of Jesus, was built there. Others contend that she was buried there, along with St David, St Patrick, twelve disciples of St Philip, King Coel (the legendary father of Constantine), King Arthur and his queen Guinevere, and a host of notables, including Joseph of Arimathea, the man who begged the crucified body of Jesus from Pontius Pilate and buried it in his own intended tomb in Jerusalem. Another legend of Joseph of Arimathea tells how he planted his staff in the ground at Glastonbury where it became a living thorn tree. An

125

obvious characteristic of Glastonbury is that its ruined church stands upon the longest east–west line in England, from Baggy Point in the west to St Margaret's at Cliffe in the east.

What can these names tell us? 'Baggy' comes from the Norman French *baggit*, meaning a salmon that has spawned; 'Margaret' means 'pearl', the icon of wisdom. In mythological parlance, with this terrestrial line, we have a depiction of the fish-and-ring story: the newborn fish starts at one end of the significant line and, with help from the Fisherman (St Peter) at Glastonbury, finds – or becomes – the pearl at the other end. The line depicts a journey of discovery or fulfilment. Ancient Christians would have had no difficulty in identifying 'a little fish' as one baptised into their faith. As if to emphasise the deliberate construction of the Glastonbury Line, the surveyors placed Maiden Bradley Church five Survey Units from St Mary's Chapel at Glastonbury, on the line and due east of it; one further Survey Unit eastwards, still on the line, they placed Brixton Deverill Church. William Benson, then, was making a statement with his gatehouse that he controlled the flow of souls passing along the Milky Way.

The stories of Joseph of Arimathea are usually treated as legends or dodgy history; but if they are regarded as mythology – parables containing important information – they can tell us what the fish-and-ring line represents and what is the mythological significance of Glastonbury. It should be clear by now that Joseph's staff is a depiction of the Tree of Life, reaching from earth to heaven, fashioned from a thorn tree. Far from being the pathetic specimen of hawthorn on Wearyall Hill foisted on us by folklorists, the Glastonbury thorn is truly a blackthorn (*Prunus spinosa*) for, unlike its cousin on the hill (*Crataegus oxycantha*), *P. spinosa* produces its blossom before the leaves appear. It then displays what a Tree of Life is supposed to represent: a crown composed of a canopy of brilliant stars.

Let's carry the analogy of the blackthorn a little further. Its fruit is the round, black, shiny, sour sloe. Having found it we may believe that we have discovered the beautiful pearl that we sought. In truth, the true inner white kernel containing the seed of new life is not recovered without first tasting of the fruit of bitterness. That is what life teaches us.

The purpose of Joseph of Arimathea in the Gospels is to furnish a tomb for Jesus. It was in this tomb that Jesus experienced a heavenly resurrection. Joseph's tomb then achieves symbolic importance for all Christians, who believe that they also will be transformed by death. Entrance to the mythical tomb, and departure from it, must be achieved by passing through a symbolic portal, having first been baptised as a 'little fish', which, from the fundamental nature of its function, is of supreme importance. In literature, the portal is called 'the Pearly Gates' because the soul is poetically transformed into a pearl by passing through them. The mythical function of Joseph of Arimathea at Glastonbury, and his legendary burial there, is recited to indicate that he transported in myth his only referenced biblical belonging to Glastonbury – his tomb. Glastonbury Abbey, the church of St Peter and St Paul, is the symbolic tomb of Jesus, the Pearly Gates. St Peter was their guardian. The saints, kings and dignitaries who were buried there hoped thereby to get a head start on the rest of us when passing through.

The edge of the celestial Milky Way 'sits' on the star Betelgeuse, the right shoulder of Orion, although the Galactic Equator does not, passing Betelgeuse about seven degrees to the north-west. In myth, the Milky Way was sometimes composed of the sparks from the anvil of the blacksmith Chedalion, who perched on the shoulder of Orion. The Galactic Equator, or some closely approximated great circle, can be taken as a linear representation of the Milky Way (remember that we are dealing with a narrow, ragged band of light and so need something definite from which to measure) and it can only be this circle that the line through Glastonbury is intended to represent; for, in conformity with the pattern in the heavens, it passes some 700 yards north of Micheldever Church, the analogue of Betelgeuse. On earth, as in heaven, the Milky Way 'sits' on the shoulder of Orion. And as the Queen of Heaven, the constellation of Cassiopeia ('the big W') sits on the Milky Way, so the Christian Queen of Heaven, St Mary, occupies this east–west 'Glastonbury Line' at St Mary's Chapel at Glastonbury. As its name implies, in myth the Milky Way is the stream of milk, issuing from the Virgin's breast, that nourishes and sustains the souls who form the individual stars of the bright band.

The mythological theme of a giant bearing the stars is familiar from images of the primordial Titan, Atlas, who was condemned by Zeus to carry the heavens on his shoulders as punishment for the Titans' war against the Olympians. Atlas is shown in art as bearing the globe of the universe (not of the earth, as some recent images would have it).

Mythology provides other analogies for the Milky Way, including a flock of sheep. Babylonian and Sumerian texts identify their kings as Good Shepherds, and such is the case for the mythical giant Gilgamesh, both mighty hunter and good shepherd. Some scholars view this dual role as indicating a pastoral society with its eyes still set on its more primitive hunter-gatherer past. Orion the mighty hunter becomes Orion the shepherd. The celestial image confirms the notion, for not only does Orion bear his flock on his shoulders, as is

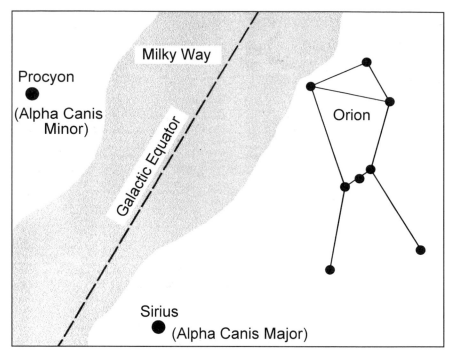

Orion 'bearing' the Milky Way, with his two 'sheep dogs', Sirius and Procyon.

familiar from early Christian iconography, but he is assisted in his task of flock management by two sheep dogs – Sirius, alpha star of the constellation Canis Major, and Procyon, alpha star of Canis Minor – one either side of the Milky Way, confining the flock to a ribbon of movement.

All these mythological references contain the common image, inspired by the pattern of the stars, of Orion supporting the Milky Way on his shoulder. This configuration is faithfully reproduced by the Orion of Wessex 'bearing' a unique geographical line that has been sanctified with the most holy Christian shrine in England. Such correspondence and complexity can leave no doubt that the 'Glastonbury Line' is an analogue of the Milky Way, and that the terrestrial Orion is not some fortuitous arrangement of churches but a deliberate plan located in a particular place and to a specific orientation.

The second mythological strand of 'bearing' relates to the four pillars supporting the heavens, such as are present in the tomb of St Sebald, and deriving from the biblical 'four corners of the earth' (Isaiah 11:12) or from the four pillars of the tabernacle that held up the cloth of blue, purple and crimson representing the sky over the Holy of Holies (Exodus 26:32). In this case, the 'pillars' would be well represented by the stars Saiph, Rigel, Betelgeuse and Bellatrix (Orion's 'corner' stars); the virtues of the four pillars would then be Wisdom, Enlightenment, Strength and Justice – not a bad choice of virtues on which to found a moral philosophy.

The River Eridanus

The River Eridanus, a long, straggling constellation of stars, weaves its tortuous way southwards through many other constellations. It is unique among them in this property. Its alpha star, Achernar, from the Arabic 'star at the end of the river', is the southernmost of Eridanus' bright stars and lies next to the constellation Phoenix. It can be observed only from more southerly latitudes. For example, in 330 BC it could be seen briefly appearing on the horizon (at 1800 hours local time at the winter solstice and at midnight on the autumnal equinox) at latitude 20.5 degrees north; this limiting latitude has been moving southwards since. The rising of Phoenix precedes Achernar's appearance. Phoenix seems to be incubating the egg Achernar, which gives birth to … itself. The myth of the phoenix is of Arabian origin, and the rising of the constellation and Achernar could (and still can) be seen from southern Arabia. Early Christians are said to have believed in the literal truth of the pre-Christian myth of the phoenix; certainly, it appeared as a symbol of the Resurrection in Christian art for hundreds of years. For them, and for their pagan forbears, there must have existed a symbolic mechanism for a soul to reach Achernar for this rebirth to take place. As *Hamlet's mill* has it, Eridanus fulfilled the galactic function of linking the inhabited world with the abode of the dead in the celestial south. It is conjectured by scholars that Eridanus received this role because, owing to the precession of the equinoxes, the Milky Way – which had long fulfilled this mythical function of a bridge for 'souls' between heaven and earth – had moved its relative position in the skies; that bridge had been broken. In fact, the constellation as now defined has been lengthened by astronomers so that 'the river' stretches to Achernar. In every country subscribing to this mythology, there is a terrestrial river, designated as sacred, that is deemed to join with the celestial Eridanus when it reaches the sea. Earthly souls migrate down the terrestrial watery river directly into the celestial river, either to become golden points in the sky (stars) or to reach the constellation of Phoenix where they are reborn in a manner similar to the creator god creating himself – a kind of auto-resurrection.

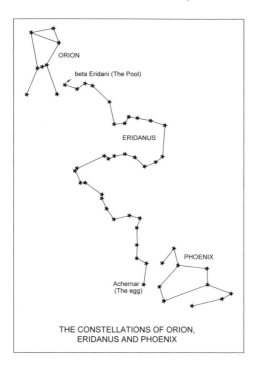

ORION

beta Eridani (The Pool)

ERIDANUS

PHOENIX

Achernar
(The egg)

THE CONSTELLATIONS OF ORION,
ERIDANUS AND PHOENIX

There is one Greek myth regarding the Eridanus that we should particularly note. The youth Phaëton seeks out his father, Apollo, who is driving the carriage of the sun, and persuades Apollo, against his better judgement, to let him take a turn at steering it. Apollo gives his son instructions but they are ignored; the horses bolt and Phaëton falls into the River Eridanus, scorched to death. Zeus turns Phaëton's sisters, the Heliades, into poplar trees on the banks of the river, where they weep tears of amber into the waters. The fifth-century BC Athenian tragedian Euripides mentions this colourful lacrimation in his play *Hippolytus*; the passage is followed by a reference to Atlas guarding the pillar 'beyond which men may not pass', which is located on the shore where apples grow. Euripides' audience would have understood the allusion to Atlas' realm of Atlantis where grew the golden apples of the Hesperides. It is easy to forget this first function of Atlas as guardian of the pillar; more memorable is his eternal penance, for siding with the Olympians in their war, of supporting the universe, although he still retained responsibility for the safety of the golden apples. Ultimately, some scholars claim, Atlas became regarded as the personification of the Cosmic Axis. The Pythagoreans attributed the formation of the Milky Way to a star dislodged and shattered by Phaëton's wild ride.

Eridanus was linked in antiquity with several major terrestrial rivers, including the Po, the Euphrates, the Rhône, the Nile and the Ganges. It was common to suppose that the terrestrial rivers each had its source in Paradise. Here is the acid test of the meaningfulness of the pattern on the ground discovered so far. Can we discover a real river in southern England that would serve unequivocally as the terrestrial part of the mythical Eridanus? It would need to rise in an identifiable Paradise; to bear a connotation of golden specks representing souls borne along by its current; and to join the celestial river at an identifiable point both consistent with the mythology and mirroring the pattern in the heavens. These are tough conditions to impose; but if they can be met, there can be no doubting that the pattern has been devised as a consistent whole.

There are two snippets of information that may help in the search. First, the Hindus considered Orion to be a representation of Vishnu, their Supreme Being. The constellation of Eridanus springs from his foot, represented by the star Rigel. In other cultures, the Eridanus sprang not from Rigel, but from its beta-star, Cursa, known more widely as The Pool, lying just above Orion's left foot. Secondly, the Egyptian Coptic Christians considered St Michael to be the guardian of the River Nile, the Egyptian Eridanus.

The Wessex Orion stands with his left foot – Moreton Church (Rigel) – on the bank of the River Frome. Identifying on the ground where the beta star of Eridanus, The Pool, should lie in relation to Moreton Church, we find the town of Poole, lying on the edge of Poole Harbour. Could there be a better analogue? Poole Harbour is one of the largest in the world, but too shallow to be developed for modern ships. It contains a number of islands, the largest by far being Brownsea Island, which sits commandingly in the harbour, like an egg in a nest, a fine example of a liminal territory. Here the waters of the land become the waters of the sea: fresh and salt water commingle. In this liminal fluid, neither riverine nor oceanic but a meld of both, like an egg awaiting birth, lies the sandy space that is both the souls' last port on earth and their springboard to the sky. They arrive in Poole Harbour by flowing down the terrestrial Eridanus of Wessex, the River Frome. The name 'Frome', pronounced locally as 'Froom', derives from the Latin *frume* (compare the French *froment*) meaning 'wheat' or more generally 'grain'. Those who seek a Celtic origin of the name produce the equally acceptable 'fair' or 'golden'. Down the Frome, figuratively, flow the golden grains, like the amber tears of Phaëton's sad sisters, past the left foot of Orion at Moreton, and enter the estuary within the harbour. The end of the Frome and the beginning of Poole

Harbour is marked by the line of the Cosmic Axis, which cuts through a point on the shore named Gold Point.

Very oddly, our eighteenth-century villain, William Benson, bought the castle on Brownsea Island, conducting esoteric nocturnal rituals there. Was he seeking to demonstrate that, in addition to his gatehouse on the 'Milky Way', his castle exercised control over the souls flowing down the Eridanus?

The most important religious city of ancient Sumeria, and probably the oldest one, Eridu, was built on a sandy island in the River Euphrates, near to the sea. Alluvial deposits over many millennia mean that it now lies well inland. Archaeology has shown that Eridu contained a long sequence of superpositioned temples, the earliest a single-roomed structure. The city was home to Enki, lord of the earth and the sweet waters, the god of learning, arts and science, creator of humankind. 'Eridu' is understood to mean the 'confluence of the rivers'. The present situation where the Tigris and the Euphrates join to form the Shaat-al-Arab obscures the fact that they were not conjoined in the heyday of Eridu, in the Ubaid period. The word 'confluence' must then be understood as the flowing together of the terrestrial and astral components of the Eridanus, whose name can now be surmised to mean 'the outflowing of the confluence of the waters'.

It is tempting, and would be reasonable, to regard Brownsea Island as a mythological analogue of the city of Eridu, and the Frome as a model for the Euphrates. If this were the case, Moreton Church, Orion's left foot, stands as a passable analogue of the city of Ur of the Chaldees, home of the fabled astronomers and of Abraham, making the patriarch yet another candidate for the terrestrial Orion; but there is no additional supporting evidence that I can discover for this attractive conjecture.

The Garden of Eden

Few people throughout history have had difficulties in accepting 'Paradise' as an alternative name for the Garden of Eden, the reason being that the word 'paradise' is of Persian origin and meant a walled garden or royal hunting park, similar to the Greeks' Elysian Fields, the final home of heroes and saints. Jesus claimed that his Father's house had many mansions (John 14:2); and the second-century church father St Irenaeus, using this plurality of possibilities, wrote that souls not damned would be dispatched to one of three places: heaven, paradise, or the restored Jerusalem. We must take heart from this explanation, because we have already found soul-places at analogues of Valhalla, Jerusalem and the Milky Way. Multiple residences accord with religious doctrine; they are to be expected in a pattern increasingly being revealed as one dealing with the themes of death, resurrection and spiritual destiny.

The interest in the Garden of Eden arises from the suggestion that all holy rivers have their sources in Paradise. The pivotal question is: does the source of the River Frome lie in Paradise? If so, having traced the river to its source, how might we unambiguously identify the area as the Garden of Eden? What should be there to make the identification unequivocal?

The Book of Genesis tells us that Eden was a garden. Two trees grew in it: the Tree of the Knowledge of Good and Evil, and the Tree of Life. The former tree lay at the centre of the garden and bore fruit that conferred this knowledge to the eater, although eating it was proscribed by God. A wily serpent lived at the centre, too, where it persuaded Eve to eat the fruit. One unnamed river rose in Eden, which branched into four on leaving the garden: the Tigris, the Euphrates, the Pishon and the Gihon. God placed an angel with a sword outside the garden, on its eastern side, to prevent Adam and Eve eating the fruit of the Tree of Life, and so becoming immortal, when they had been expelled from Eden. This action seems to contradict the fact that the Tree of Life is stated to lie within the garden.

The notion of centrality has caused the Garden of Eden to be regarded in subsequent myth as circular, in accordance with the perception that a circle is the perfect shape. Non-biblical mythology also altered the image of the Garden. The Tree of Knowledge of Good and Evil became a more generalised Tree of Knowledge, and its identity became fused with that of the Tree of Life, possibly to resolve the inside/outside ambiguity noted above. In Norse mythology, Mimir was a primal god who owned a well of knowledge, which watered one of the roots of the Tree of Life/Knowledge, Yggrdasil, upon which Woden hung for nine days to gain wisdom and knowledge; a further price for these gifts entailed Woden plucking out one eye, which fell into the well of Mimir. Later, Mimir's enemies cut off his head, which Woden preserved and kept so that it could advise and inform him when necessary. The idea that the Tree of Knowledge in the Garden of Eden was watered by a stream of knowledge is depicted in medieval woodcuts.

Here, then, are many properties and characteristics of potential use in deciding whether or not the countryside around the source of the River Frome is a model of the Garden of Eden.

First, note that the terrestrial source of the celestial River Eridanus is a pool – Poole Harbour. For consistency, then, the source of the terrestrial Eridanus,

St John's Well, Evershot, the source of the River Frome. (*Author's image*)

the Frome, should also rise in a pool, possibly one with some kind of sacred context. This is not a common characteristic of rivers in general; in fact, it is rare. The River Frome must therefore be special, for its source is St John's Well, lying near the church of St Osmund in the Dorset village of Evershot. The church lies one Survey Unit from a labyrinthine miz-maze in a field near the village of Leigh. The direction is that of midsummer's sunrise. The path of the labyrinth has decayed beyond visibility, but the surrounding hexagonal bank remains intact. Recall that traversing the labyrinth imparts wisdom; it, then, is a recognisable and tangible 'fruit'. For biblical consistency, it needs to lie at the centre of the Garden of Eden. That is where the snake dwelt, too, a creature of sin in Christian theology, but one of wisdom in other cultures; and what is a labyrinth but a snake coiled in cunning fashion? Our wily serpent speaks with a Dorset accent.

To repeat the conclusion: the Tree of Knowledge is represented by a midsummer's line one Survey Unit in length from Evershot Church to Leigh Miz-maze; its fruit is the labyrinth, and its roots are watered by the holy well of St John the Baptist.

William Shakespeare, in *A Midsummer Night's Dream*, writes:

134

> The nine men's morris is fill'd up with mud;
>
> And the quaint mazes in the wanton green,
>
> For lack of tread are undistinguishable.

These lines, spoken by Titania, convey the impression, still purveyed in uncritical works, that labyrinths were some type of bucolic play park, where children disported themselves in merry prances of a fine summer's evening. Breamore Miz-maze lies in remote countryside, and Leigh Miz-maze sits on top of a low hill in fields 500 yards from the village centre: no 'wanton greens' here. Whatever games of sport or witchcraft were subsequently played on these two particular labyrinths, their original purpose was of a much more esoteric and serious nature than childish frolicks.

Due east of Leigh Miz-maze, at exactly one Survey Unit, lies the church of St Mary the Virgin at Glanvilles Wootton (prior to 1985, named Wootton Glanville). It seems that the earthly model of Paradise possesses exactly the same shape and dimensions as the world model centred on the Rufus Stone. According to legend, Glanvilles Wootton Church was originally a chantry chapel founded as a penance by disobedient hunters who had killed a favourite white hart of Henry II (reigned 1154–1189). Some ancient and beautiful encaustic tiles within the church tell the story pictorially. Paradise was indeed a royal hunting park.

There is some significance to Glanvilles Wootton Church standing due east of the centre of the garden. Following the layouts of old cities with their gateways positioned at the four cardinal points, we can surmise that it also marked a gateway. The Garden of Eden certainly had an exit, for Adam and Eve were expelled through it. With a broad enough view, they would see in Wessex a gigantic image of Orion lying to the east, brandishing his sword, standing in front of the Tree of Life.

Here, we encounter a problem. Another church almost lies on the circle of Paradise: Frome St Quintin; it is about 170 yards inside the circle (an error of 2.6 per cent). The radial path from Leigh Miz-maze passes over a large tract of very hilly ground, which may account for the discrepancy; there is nothing to guide us as to whether 'a circle' was deemed to have consisted of a ring, such as might be indicated by a template being placed over a map, or whether its irregular 'circumference' was defined by a series of standard radii measured on the undulating ground surface. The problem did not arise in the New Forest, because all the radii were on relatively flat ground. The church of Frome St Quintin has symbolic importance relevant to the circle of Paradise so, while it would be improper to 'force it into position', information would be lost by excluding it without good reason. The position is further complicated, because the church lies precisely one Celestial Unit from Glanvilles Wootton Church, despite some comparably hilly ground intervening, and this layout justifies recording the evidence of Frome St Quintin Church that follows.

St Quintin was an Italian Christian missionary active in Picardy. He was persecuted and tortured, being thrown into gaol, where an angel appeared and engineered his miraculous release. He was arrested again and beheaded on 31 October AD 287. His body was thrown into a marsh, but discovered on 24 June and buried on 3 January. The cathedral of St Quentin was erected over his tomb; its nave is paved with a labyrinth. These mythical events mirror the life and death of John the Baptist, even down to the saint's first *inventio* (the date of the discovery of his body) being made to coincide with St John's Day. The cult of St Quintin became very popular in northern France during the Middle Ages. There are no other church dedications to St Quintin in England (the church at Stanton St Quintin is dedicated to St Giles) so what is St Quintin's church at Frome doing just inside Paradise in Dorset?

The answer could lie with the de Glanville family, whose home was at Glanville, near Pont Évêque in Normandy. Randulph de Glanville fought alongside Duke William at the Battle of Hastings, and was created Baron de Bromham as a reward. The Glanville family remained prominent and powerful: Henry became chamberlain to King Stephen; Randulph, Lord Chief Justice of England in 1172, and governor of Winchester Castle, joined the Third Crusade and died before the walls of Acre while fighting Saladin's forces in 1191. Henry de Glanville held the Lordship of Wootton Glanville in 1213, a hereditary position that lasted for at least another three generations. The Norman knights picked up new esoteric ideas while on their Crusades in the Middle East; it is likely that the Glanvilles added these to their home cult of St Quintin and imported them into Dorset, along with that saint's esoteric attributes, which included midsummer aspects (through Quintin's surrogacy of John the Baptist) and the symbol of the labyrinth. This hypothesis is in line with the Norman French name, Frome, and the origin of the name Baggy Point at the western end of the 'Milky Way'. But the symbolism of Dorset's Garden of Eden fits so comfortably, too, with the Saxon mythology of Woden and Yggdrasil, and with Mimir. To the Glanvilles, the Mimir/Quintin/St John equivalence would have been a natural one. As new masters of England, the Normans became heirs to an ancient system of symbolism, but they could only add to it, rename it, and reinterpret features of it. It has outlived them and many other dynasties.

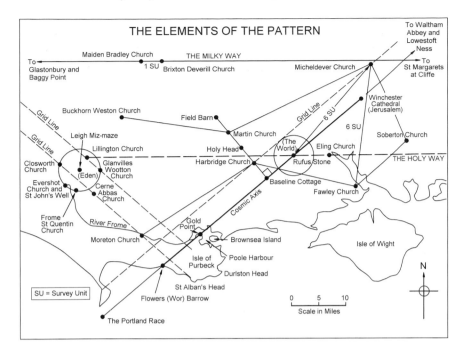

Their additions have had two effects. Usefully, they make the pattern more visible, but their widening of the mythological context renders the process of interpretation that much more difficult. As local elements of the pattern change symbolic emphasis over time, under the control of fresh cultural and personal preferences, so the mythological consistency of the whole becomes less amenable to certain forensic analysis. For instance, Paradise is a destination for good souls, but the Garden of Eden is an embarkation point for sinful humans. When the two are made equivalent, there is a contradiction, a bifurcation of mythologies caused by a plurality of differing cultural owners. For example, on the one hand, we have developed a clear model of the Garden of Eden, but the Holy Way, which leads to Paradise, terminates at St Andrew's Church in Lillington, within the circle.

Different perceptions of the association between the circle of Paradise and Orion can also be imagined. We have discussed the 'Garden of Eden and sword-wielding angel' relationship. Readily apparent, too, is the springing of the newborn Orion from his ox hide filled with urine; the golden stream of the River Frome sits well with this particular image. A river of grain issuing from the periphery of the circle at Evershot suggests a threshing floor, perhaps the one that David bought at its proper market price upon which to build the 'Temple of Solomon'; does Solomon, as Orion, stand guard over his temple?

Sacred rivers and severed heads

The gruesome cult of the severed head appears in stark contrast to the intellectual business of delineating mathematical ratios, but the notion that the head was the seat of the soul permeated all philosophical systems of the time. Its realisation in the head of Harold at Waltham, atop the stake of the Cosmic Axis, was one of the clues to the existence of the terrestrial pattern of celestial dispositions. In the following chapter, more heads will appear in relation to the general model established here of a rotating axis with midsummer connections and a head or pole at its summit, guarded by a giant.

The versatility of the Orion/Eden/Frome combination extends also to the Woden iconography. Woden, with his one remaining eye (Meissa, Soberton Church) can be seen as 'hanging' on the Cosmic Axis, in which case Leigh Miz-maze could be his sacrificial eye that fell into the Well of Mimir. The geometric tendency of pictorial symbolism dictates that the eye would lie in the centre of a circular well: there is nothing revolutionary in this assumption. The remaining element is the sacred river; it must be accommodated in the pattern.

Sacred rivers were of particular importance to the Celts, and the interest persisted with the Saxons. For example, the sacred River Thames was known to the Celts as Tamesa and by the Saxons as Temes, a clear case of continuity of religious regard. Dr Anne Ross (*Pagan Celtic Britain*) writes that springs, wells and rivers are the chief focal points of Celtic cult practices. She cites the temple to the goddess Sequanna, which the Celts located at the source of the river Seine, and which was reinstated with a 'nymph of the grot' by Napoleon III. Ross also writes of the extent to which the Celts venerated the severed head as a symbol within their religion and as a motif in their art. She notes how the cult of the severed head was bound up with all other cults, especially that of sacred waters, particularly wells, citing the legend of St Melor, whose severed head spoke and produced a spring of clear water whenever the staff upon which it was impaled was thrust into the earth. Ross gives instances from literature where the Celts kept heads in wells. She also points out that the Christian Church embraced the cult, making Celtic sacred wells centres for the cults of local saints; she considers this practice as convincing evidence of the 'unbroken continuity' of religious ideas from Celtic times into the Christian era. However, the persistent need for a supply of efficacious holy water in an age of only primitive medical practice could account for such continuity.

A modern Humbaba mask in string, based on an original in the British Museum. (*Author's image*)

All arguments considered, it is natural to find St John the Baptist associated with a well that is the source of a Celtic sacred river, the Frome. This well lies exactly one Survey Unit (6561 yards) from Leigh Miz-maze, which is the centre of a circle that could represent the Well of Mimir, possibly containing the eye of Woden. The inference, then, is that Mimir's Well is the mythic source of the River Frome, and that St John's Well acts as a kind of spigot, the source of the real water, tapping the tub of fabulous well water produced by it. Put another way, the labyrinth at Leigh produces wisdom or knowledge that fills Paradise and distils into physical water as it spills into the real world under the authority and protection of John the Baptist.

The question is at once raised: how likely is it that the natural source of the River Frome should lie conveniently 6561 yards from a small hill, a suitable spot on which to construct a labyrinth? The answer is: not at all. St John's Well must have been dug in a precisely surveyed spot, so that it now lies on the circumference of Mimir's Well; the source of the Frome lay nearby, but was redefined by this action to fit mythological requirements. The notion of the labyrinth serving as Mimir's head is supported by ancient evidence: Gilgamesh killed a fire-breathing giant named Humbaba whose face was depicted as composed of intestines arranged in a suitably labyrinthine form to represent the head's several features. The wily serpent assumes yet another guise.

Recollections

This is perhaps the point to remind ourselves that our journey began in ignorance at the Rufus Stone, the centre of a circle representing the material world, and it has ended at the centre of an identical circle representing spiritual Paradise, contemplating one of the most ancient of images, a symbol of knowledge, albeit one of guts and terror.

9

FAINT ECHOES?

If I have caused one man to look upwards I have fulfilled my purpose.
Translation of words found on an old astrolabe

The end of an era?

We have been discovering faint echoes of a philosophy that was once vibrant and assertive, one with the energy and the drive to map its symbolic view of god, mankind and the heavens onto the landscape of southern England. That impulse and conviction had come together at least once before on the same territory and produced Stonehenge, a massive feat of civil engineering absorbing huge resources, exacting universal compliance, and demanding respect and awe. Over two millennia separate the projects but they share common features, solstitial attributes and circular patterns. The continuity of sun-based theology throughout ancient Egypt, up to the end of the Roman era, supplies sufficient explanation for the similar solar references found in both Stonehenge and the Wessex pattern, despite the ages separating them; Egypt provided a continuing esoteric curriculum for Europe and western Asia, although some of the main themes were not original ones: there were national indigenous elements.

But as we saw with the notion of harmonies, the Renaissance renewed the interest of thinking men in anciently discovered doctrines. But the Middle Ages were not entirely barren of the old philosophies. We have examined the tomb of St Sebald. More generally, the art historian Anthony Blunt (*Artistic theory in Italy 1450–1500*) writes of Christian attitudes to Classical themes during the Renaissance, explaining how pagan doctrines and symbols were adopted by Christianity. These practices, says Blunt, were actively encouraged by the popes from Nicholas V (pope from 1447) to Clement VII (pope until 1534).

Blunt also refers to the influential work by the didactic analyst Lomazzo, *Idea del tempio della pictura*, published in Milan in 1590. Lomazzo was heavily influenced by astrology, and constructed a complex system of symbolism in which every aspect of a painting falls under the influence of a specific planet. He also developed a system of number symbolism incorporating his astrological beliefs, including, for example, the seven circles of heaven.

Denis Cosgrove ('The geometry of landscape' in *The iconography of landscape)* articulated the commonality of expression between Renaissance paintings and the vastly wider and more permanent canvas of landscape, noting that geometry – essential to cartography and architecture – also formed a core part of neo-platonic cosmology and its related mythology, and from there percolated the art of the period.

Here, then, is the complete description of the process of structuring paintings according to symbolic astronomical rules displaying an epistemology coeval with late Roman Wessex. How strange, therefore, to find a past curator of the British Museum asserting on television that of the two million drawings and prints owned by that institution not one displayed this type of symbolism. Had he analysed them all?

Secret astronomical symbolism was incorporated into sixteenth-century paintings, as has been firmly established by John North's analysis of a painting by Hans Holbein the Younger (see *The ambassadors' secret*). My example is Titian's *Venus and Adonis*, which hangs in the National Gallery and was painted in the middle of the sixteenth century. Venus is depicted in an uncomfortable and unnatural attitude, imploring Adonis to tarry for lovemaking. Remarkably, Venus's ankles, knees, hips, shoulders and visible elbow represent nine stars of Virgo; the crown of her head marks Spica, the alpha star of the constellation. As remarkable is the fact that when the ecliptic is drawn relative to these stars, it passes through the visible eyes of both Venus and Adonis. Adonis is, naturally, following the sun that is in constant motion. He cannot stay with Venus: the sun cannot stop.

The painting is a copy of one that hung in the Vatican. Why was it painted and who paid for it, and why is the sexually active Venus associated with the constellation of the Virgin? In their motion round the ecliptic at different speeds the sun and Venus briefly coincide five times every eight years. On 30 September 1560 (by modern reckoning) they lay together in the head of Virgo,

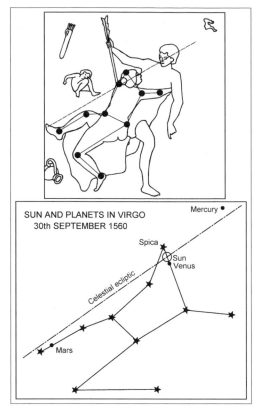

SUN AND PLANETS IN VIRGO
30th SEPTEMBER 1560

Mercury

Spica

Sun
Venus

Celestial ecliptic

Mars

A comparison of the essential elements of Titian's *Venus and Adonis* in the National Gallery with a portion of the heavens on 30 September 1560.

near Spica; behind them lay Mars and ahead shone Mercury in the process of performing an apparent loop in his orbit. Both these planets are visible in the painting (although they were too near the sun to be observable in the sky): Mercury as an indistinct figure in the top right-hand corner, and Mars, asleep, over Venus's right knee, his quiver hung in a tree. Allegorically, peace reigns because warlike Mars is asleep. Undoubtedly, though, he is doubling as a neglectful Cupid who fails to awaken love in Adonis. This particular configuration of planets is unique to the year 1560. To answer our questions, it would appear that Venus can renew her virginity by coinciding with the Virgin, as is shown by the intact pot (in art, broken pots are symbolic of lost virginity) lying by her left foot, which also confirms the indifference and 'innocence' of Adonis. The original painting was almost certainly commissioned to mark the coronation of Pius IV, a member of the Medici family who was elected pope in December 1559. However, it is claimed that the canvas in the National Gallery is a studio copy made for Philip II of Spain in 1554.

The pose of Venus is strikingly similar to one in another painting of Mars and Venus displayed in the National Gallery, by Jacopo Palma (Palma Giovane) who, as has been noted, painted a *groma* in an allegorical setting. These pictures confirm the importance of astronomical (or astrological) features, including the invisible ecliptic, in religious thought. They form documentary evidence, no less than does the written word, that an ancient skein of philosophy re-emerged re-energised during the Renaissance, affirming its ubiquitous existence in the linked fields of art, metaphysics and astronomy.

But then it was lost from view. It cannot have been a victim of the dawning age of enlightenment, for even now there are more people disposed to beliefs in spooks and spirits than engage in consistent rational thought – more than enough to maintain such a potent symbol. Or did the symbol lose its potency? Or was it deliberately hidden from view? Whatever the answer to these questions, and they will not be addressed here, it is unlikely that the Wessex pattern on its own spawned the international awareness of the basic symbol of rotating Cosmic Axis, crowning emblem, and guardian giant that the examples presented here display. I am not equipped to examine landscapes other than my own, so I shall present a further three examples from the countryside with which I am familiar. They are not so detailed as the one based on the Rufus Stone, but they do demonstrate the generality and continuity of the idea.

A sceptred isle

The Romans' name for the Isle of Wight was *Insula Vectis*, which translates as the 'Island of the Pillar' (specifically, a supporting pillar). The base of the notional pillar stands on the cliff-top at St Catherine's Hill, on the southern coast of the island. St Catherine's symbol is the flaming solar disc that derives from the wheel upon which she was martyred. This device imparts symbolic rotation to the pillar, which reaches to Colchester, the chief town of the Celts in the east of the country; as their major garrison, it became the nearest thing that the Romans had to a capital city in Britain. By claiming Colchester, at the top of the pillar, as their own, the Romans were proclaiming that their control of the country was endorsed by heaven. The revolt of the Celts under Queen Boudicca of the Iceni tribe in AD 60 focused on the attack of Colchester, which they burned to the ground, not simply for military reasons; occupation of it possessed a deep symbolic importance for both sides, much as the successful defence of Stalingrad against Nazi invaders possessed for Stalin and the Russian people, and as the defeat and occupation of Berlin by the Red Army did subsequently.

The giant of St Catherine's Hill survives in legend only, as a capricious, rock-hurling belligerent, but he is there. The line of the 'pillar' cuts through the Thames Estuary at a town named Erith, possibly indicating that the River Eridanus – alias Britain's largest river, the Thames – is included in the mythological scheme.

It is possible, in this example, that we are witnessing an early attempt to survey a countrywide *cardo* across Roman Britain, a symbolic representation of a major highway through every Roman city and military camp.

Almost a carbon copy

A remarkable summer solstice line is aligned with six churches, those of Ogbourne St Andrew, Warminster's St Denys' Minster, Horningsham, Cadbury Castle, South Cadbury, and Marston Magna. The line passes through

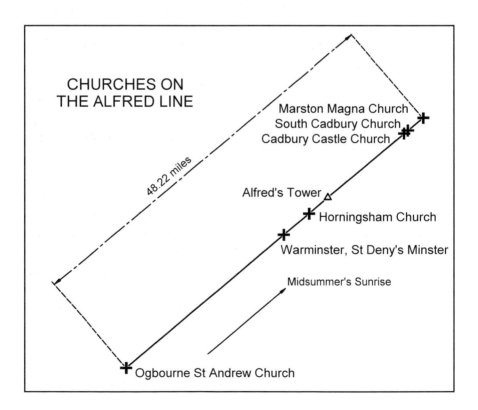

Alfred's Tower, Somerset. (*Author's image*)

Wantage, where Alfred the Great was born, according to his teacher and biographer, Bishop Asser. On this line, on Kingsettle Hill, Henry Hoare II, a banker, owner of Stourhead estate and a Freemason, completed Alfred's Tower in 1772. The folly is 160 feet high and triangular in cross section, a prominent landmark overlooking much of Wiltshire and Somerset. It stands on the solstitial line just described, on the site of the Egbert Stone, where legend has it King Alfred rallied his forces to fight against the Vikings. Like Winchester, the Iron Age hill-fort of Cadbury Castle is frequently identified with Camelot, the legendary court of King Arthur. Like the Cosmic Axis through the Rufus Stone, there are severed human heads associated with this 'Alfred Line', one at 'Camelot', where Sir Gawayne struck off the head of the Green Knight, who promptly picked it up and rode off with it; another at Horningsham, where the church is dedicated to the decapitated John the Baptist (who, as we are well aware, also has summer solstice connections); and yet another at Warminster, which is dedicated to St Denys, the patron saint of France, who was fabled to have carried his head from his place of execution at Montmartre to that of his burial. We should note that the element 'wor' evident in 'Warminster' denotes 'spinning', comparable with the 'win' of 'Winchester', which was, of course, Alfred's capital.

As with the Cosmic Axis, the terrestrial origin of the Alfred Line lies within a cliff-top Iron Age hill-fort, to the west of Seaton, at Branscombe in this case. Is this not a strange parallel? Two spinning solstitial lines are aligned on religious buildings, with a realisation of Camelot lying on each, and each possessing associations with decapitations. Each contains a stone named after a king, and each has a triangular structure on it, both associated with eminent Freemasons around the middle of the eighteenth century.

A couple of hours spent on the Internet reveals the likely reason for the triangular monuments. The Noahites (Prussian Knights) became a hugely popular Masonic degree in the eighteenth century. Noah threatened to displace Hiram as the central Masonic character. Initiates met only in remote locations at full moon. The degree's storyline involved Phaleg (or Peleg), descendant of Noah and ancestor of Abraham, being disgraced for suggesting the building of the Tower of Babel to ensure survival during a future Deluge, presumably for disrespectfully disregarding the rainbow that God caused to appear after the flood as a promise that no further inundation would occur. As a penance, Phaleg went to live alone in a delta-shaped temple built deep within the forest.

An alternative legend credits Phaleg with building triangular temples wherever he stopped on a journey round the earth. Alfred's Tower was almost certainly based on the idea of Phaleg's temple. Hoare filled his Stourhead estate with grottoes and temples dedicated to pagan gods and spirits, including a model of the temple of Apollo at Balbec. 'Phaleg' means 'divider of the land'. Before county boundaries were altered, Alfred's Tower stood on the boundary of the counties of Wiltshire and Somerset. The tower did indeed mark the division of the land, but in a different sense it united it too. Arguably, it could qualify as a Jacob's Ladder in its own right for, besides its solstitial provenance, it is guarded by a statue of the hero figure King Alfred, has a spiral (turning) staircase, and reaches far heavenwards – at least providing awesome, heavenly vistas for the pilgrim who gains the summit. Should the pilgrim's ground-based companions utter the merest whisper, it will be conveyed to the summit by the tower's central shaft, as if by a ship's speaking tube. The effect on a lone, nocturnal pilgrim could be dramatic, especially if the noises were eerie or the utterances disturbingly profound.

No royal palace has been found at Wantage, and Professor Alfred Smyth (*King Alfred the Great*) considers it extremely improbable that Alfred was born there. What is left is a powerful argument for another case of status transference, such as happened at the Rufus Stone.

Returning to Branscombe, the origin of the line, the name could denote 'the valley belonging to Brand', or 'to the ravens', but it could also be the Valley of Brân, the gigantic Celtic deity, 'crowned king over Britain'. Brân's head was severed, finally being buried on White Hill, at the Tower of London, where it provided peace and prosperity for eighty years. (The name Brân means 'raven', whence the legend that disaster will strike the fortifications and the monarchy

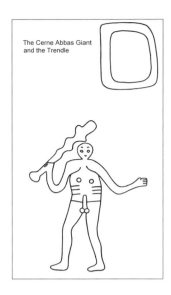

The Cerne Abbas Giant
and the Trendle

The chalk hill-figure of the Giant overlooks the village
of Cerne Abbas; its age is a matter of great debate.

if the resident ravens leave the Tower.) Note, too, that Ogbourne St Andrew's
Church derives its name from the Celtic sun god Ogmios, undoubtedly an
incarnation of the ancient Sumerian god Ugmash (Shamash) whose name in
that language means 'sun wisdom'. Ogmios is depicted in art as a Herculean
figure wielding a bow and a club. Brân and Ogmios are both credited with
creating the alphabet, and are clearly different names for the same god-hero.

The Cerne Abbas Giant of Dorset immediately comes to mind, the huge
chalk hill-figure so obviously full of vigour and aggression. He possesses his
own east–west line. It stretches from the Trendle, a rectangular earthwork
lying over the Giant's shoulder, to the remains of an immensely old oak tree in
the New Forest named the Naked Man, and then on to the ancient church of
Brockenhust, also in the New Forest. Legend has it that a highwayman named
Mark Way was hanged from the Naked Man, a clumsy attempt to present the
tree as a way-mark. Perhaps we have discovered part of another astronomical
structure, but the echoes are too faint to decipher confidently.

The naked truth

It was noted in 1901 by Sir Norman Lockyer, the then Astronomer Royal, that
the axis of Stonehenge was a solstitial one, and that its bearing was consistent
with the axis being laid out within two hundred years of 1,820 BC. Current

opinion is that the intended direction lay towards the setting midwinter's sun, just as I postulated that observers stationed at Flowers Barrow watched the midwinter's sun as it set into the Portland Race. If we set off from the centre of Stonehenge in this direction, at an azimuth of 227.89 degrees, we shall strike the Trendle, lying over the left shoulder of the Cerne Abbas Giant. Accurate calculations taking into account the refraction of the sun's rays by the atmosphere near the ground, whereby the light is effectively bent downwards, suggest that observers at Stonehenge looking on the reciprocal bearing (47.89 degrees) would have observed the first gleam of the rising midsummer's sun on the horizon in 2,800 BC. Small variations in the refraction of the light that occur from dawn to dawn, owing to the variation in weather conditions, put a tolerance on this figure of about three centuries either way, a tolerance that does not materially affect the argument that follows.

The name 'Trendle' is identical to the Old German word meaning a disc, or wheel, and is related to the later Old English word 'trundle', which means to turn around. The action of turning is thus implied both at Cerne and at Stonehenge. These two locations are the only ones on the line joining them (or its projections) that contain monuments: therefore, we can reasonably assume that they form the start and end points of the line. According to our validated model, Stonehenge, at the top of the line, is a pole or head. Only one reasonable possibility exists: Stonehenge was built as an analogue of the pole star in 2,800 BC: Thuban, the tail star of the constellation of Draco. And those who claim Stonehenge to be the place where recently departed souls were deemed to set out for heaven are correct, for the pole was the celestial portal recognised by the ancient Egyptians and others.

Incredibly, it is possible to verify that Stonehenge indeed lies on a notional pole with a declination expressed in modern terminology as 90 degrees. Following the precedent set by our model, the Trendle at Cerne must represent zero degrees. As before, the line can be divided into a linear scale, every point of which represents a declination lying between zero and 90 degrees. I concluded that the Holy Way, representative of the tropic of Cancer, was an ancient artefact because it cut the southern terminal of the Dorset Cursus. The Holy Way also cuts through the Cerne to Stonehenge line at a point representative of a declination of 23.83 degrees, at the Dorset hamlet of Broad Oak, near Sturminster Newton. This is the value of the declination of the tropic of Cancer in the third millennium BC. It is intriguing to observe how a line of latitude (50.910 degrees, in this case) can be made to represent different declinations simply by manipulating the start and end points of an axis placed

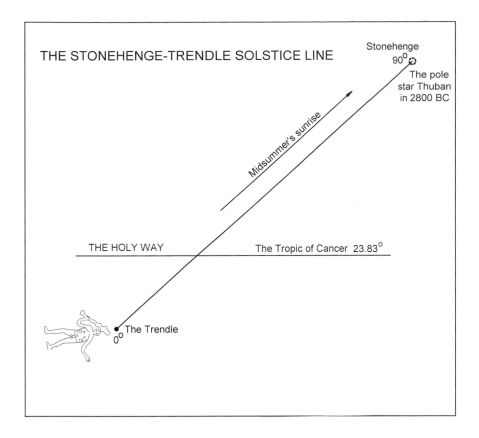

THE STONEHENGE-TRENDLE SOLSTICE LINE

Stonehenge 90°

The pole star Thuban in 2800 BC

Midsummer's sunrise

THE HOLY WAY   The Tropic of Cancer 23.83°

The Trendle 0°

across it. It seems inconceivable that such precision could be obtained in the Neolithic period, or the following Bronze Age; but it is also inconceivable that such a result could happen by chance.

Whatever the explanation, it remains that we have a midsummer's axis with its base notionally impelled by rotation, guarded by a giant, and with a pole displaying associations with souls at the summit. This is no faint echo; it is both a ringing endorsement of the purposeful nature of the Cosmic Axis and a major discovery in its own right.

The awful truth

The splendour of Stonehenge was transitory. The inexorable progress of the precession of the equinoxes was revealed when the pole star Thuban was observed to move systematically away from the celestial north pole. One can

Stonehenge, Wiltshire. (*Author's image*)

imagine the corporate concern at the first indications, the checking and re-checking of the pole and the logging of the movement of Thuban down the generations. The pillars of the sky failed, and the ladder to heaven proved faulty. The very foundations of mythology crumbled. The gods were dead. Somehow or other, the symbolic importance of Stonehenge was restored, probably by the new Beaker People with fresh ideas, who arrived around 2,500 BC, and it went on to become the awesome monument whose ruin we admire today, but not before it was abandoned for a while and then given a new identity, but one that is obscure.

Eventually, it was realised that while the stars revolved nightly about the celestial pole, the pole itself revolved once every 26,000 years or so about a point in the heavens located within the constellation of Draco where one could imagine the heart to reside on a conventional 'fleshing out' of the skeleton of stars. Today, we call this heart of the dragon the ecliptic north pole. It is the one sensibly stationary point of the heavens observable from the northern hemisphere.

It is more than conceivable that this notion of rotation about a point that is itself in a circular orbit was the basis for the Ptolemaic model of the solar system, where such a mechanism, called epicyclic motion, was employed to account for the fact that planets were observed to move in orbits that were not perfectly circular. One can see how such an idea rested on the almost sacred, fundamental and demonstrable knowledge of precession. It accounts for the vehemence with which the Catholic Church defended the Ptolemaic model against the Copernican view of a sun-centred universe, and in the process burnt books and men, and imprisoned Galileo.

When astronomers had achieved a fuller understanding of the precession of the equinoxes, they built a new symbol, the Cosmic Axis, with the ecliptic pole substituted for the celestial pole. It contained symbolism as old as Stonehenge itself, and drew on new ideas of numerology developed by the Greeks. In 21,200 years' time, nocturnal visitors to the crumbling megaliths of Stonehenge who look upwards to observe the pole star will see the ancient monument's glory resurrected by the glimmerings of the pivotal star in the Dragon's Tail. Thuban will have returned.

GLOSSARY

- **Altitude:** the angular distance from the horizon of a star or point on the celestial sphere measured along an arc at right angles to the horizon.
- **Armillary sphere:** a three-dimensional model of the celestial sphere showing the celestial equator, the poles, the ecliptic, the tropics and various notable meridians, and perhaps other features.
- **Axis:** an imaginary line running through a body about which that body rotates.
- **Azimuth:** the angular distance from true north measured clockwise on a horizontal plane of a terrestrial object or, in the case of a star or point on the celestial sphere, from the south point of the horizon to a point on it intersected by a vertical line through the star.
- **Cardo:** a major street in Roman cities and military camps, normally running from north to south, but probably skewed to the midsummer's sunrise when depicted symbolically.
- **Celestial meridian:** a great circle of the celestial sphere that passes through the celestial poles.
- **Celestial sphere:** an imagined sphere, a great many times the size of the earth and co-central with it, on whose inner surface are considered, for the purposes of measurement, to be fastened the fixed stars.
- **Celestial pole:** points north and south on the celestial sphere where it is cut by a projection of the earth's axis; the poles revolve (against the background of the fixed stars) about the ecliptic poles at an angular distance equal to the obliquity of the ecliptic (about 23½ degrees) completing one revolution in about 26,000 years owing to the precession of the equinoxes.
- **Celestial equator:** the great circle generated by the extension of the earth's equatorial plane into space cutting the celestial sphere.
- **Celestial Unit:** a distance equal to a Survey Unit multiplied by the Golden Mean, equal to 10,616 yards.
- **Conjunction:** the apparent alignment or close alignment of two astronomical bodies.
- **Constellation:** an arbitrary grouping of fixed stars often occasioned and named by its resemblance to some object, animate or otherwise, recognised by a social culture.
- **Cosmic Axis:** a great circle originating in the Portland Race and passing through the Rufus Stone, Winchester Cathedral and Waltham Abbey; also known as the Rufus Line and identified with the mythical Tree of Life.
- **Declination:** the angular distance, north or south, from the celestial equator of a star or point on the celestial sphere, measured in degrees along a celestial meridian.
- **Decumanus:** a major street in Roman cities and military camps, normally running from east to west.
- **Ecliptic pole:** points north and south on the celestial sphere where it is cut by a line through the centre of the ecliptic and lying at right angles to its plane; ecliptic poles remain sensibly static against the background of the fixed star over millennia.

- **Ecliptic:** a great circle of the celestial sphere passing through the equinoxes and inclined to the plane of the celestial equator by an angle determined by the tilt of the earth's axis of rotation to its plane of orbit (that is, the obliquity of the ecliptic, about 23½ degrees); it is the track of the sun throughout the year against the background of the fixed stars; the ecliptic intersects the celestial equator at the equinoxes.
- **Equinox:** points lying on the celestial equator where it is cut by the ecliptic; the vernal equinox is at right ascension zero hours and the autumnal equinox at right ascension twelve hours; also the times of year when the sun occupies these positions, about 21 March and 22 September respectively, when the hours of daylight and darkness are equal and the sun rises due east and sets due west.
- **First point in Aries:** another name for the vernal equinox, and always taken as zero degrees of right ascension.
- **Fixed star:** one of an arbitrary group of stars whose angular distances from one another remain sensibly constant over millennia.
- **Great circle:** a circle drawn on the surface of any sphere whose centre coincides with the centre of the sphere; it is the largest circle that can be drawn on a sphere.
- **Holy Way:** a line of latitude passing through the Rufus Stone and other notable features, possibly identified with the Royal Arch of the Sun.
- **Miz-maze:** a labyrinthine path that leads the traveller towards a central point; examples are the turf Breamore Miz-maze and those in Chartres and Sens Cathedrals; the turf-cut variety was once much more common and often known as Troy Towns.
- **Precession of the equinoxes:** the movement clockwise of the equinoxes round the celestial equator owing to a regular wobble of the earth's axis of rotation whereby it sweeps out a cone on the celestial sphere with a semi-angle of about 23½ degrees once every 26,000 years or so; it is caused by the differential gravitational effects of the sun and the moon; it results in a slow change in the celestial co-ordinates of the fixed stars when measured by declination and right ascension.
- **Right ascension:** the angular distance measured eastwards along the celestial equator from the vernal equinox to a point where it is cut by a celestial meridian passing through the point for which the measurement is required; its units are hours, minutes and seconds (and decimal fractions thereof) and run from zero to twenty-four hours; conversion to angular degrees is effected by noting that one hour of right ascension is equivalent to fifteen degrees of angular measure.
- **Royal Arch of the Sun:** a description applied by the ancient Egyptians to the path taken in the sky by the midsummer's sun; also a name of a higher degree in Freemasonry.
- **Sexagesimal:** describes the system of measuring units used in ancient Mesopotamia; every larger unit is sixty times the size of the unit proceeding it: thus seconds, minutes and degrees, still used for measuring angles; and seconds, minutes and hours, still used for measuring time.
- **Small circle:** a circle drawn on the surface of a sphere that is not a great circle.
- **Solstice:** the position on the ecliptic occupied by the sun when it possesses its farthest northerly declination (summer solstice) or most southerly declination (winter solstice); also the time of year when the noonday sun reaches its highest and lowest points in the sky, about 21 June and 22 December respectively: the longest day and the longest night.
- **Solstitial colure:** a meridian of the celestial sphere that passes through the ecliptic poles and the solstices and denotes right ascension of six hours and eighteen hours; it lies at ninety degrees to the equinoxes.
- **Survey Unit:** a distance of 6561 yards; it is a distance that a man or woman can walk in an hour and derives, in sexagesimal measure, from the height of a typical human being.
- **Zodiac:** a band of the sky centred on the ecliptic and divided into twelve parts of thirty degrees, each originally named from a constellation occupying that division and through which the sun moves over the course of a year; the precession of the equinoxes means that the constellations no longer correspond with the names of zodiacal divisions designated long ago.

BIBLIOGRAPHY

Allen, R. H. *Star names: their lore and meaning (1899)*. Reissued by Dover, 1963.

Ashmore, W. and Knapp, A. B. (eds.) *Archaeologies of landscape*. Blackwell, 1999.

Bacon, Francis. *The wisdom of the ancients (1609)*. Reissued by Cassell, n.d.

Barlow, Frank. *William Rufus*. Methuen, 1983.

Blunt, A. *Artistic theory in Italy 1450–1500*. Clarendon Press, 1962.

Budge, E. A. Wallis. *The Book of the Dead (1890)*. Reissued by University Books, Inc., 1960.

Burl, H. A. W. *Prehistoric astronomy and ritual*. Shire Publications, 1983.

Carter, Howard. *The tomb of Tutankhamen*. Sphere Books, 1972.

Charles, R. H. (trans). *The book of Enoch*. SPCK, 1977.

Chrétien de Troyes. *Arthurian romances*. Dent, 1982.

Coates, Richard. *The place-names of Hampshire*. Batsford, 1989.

Cochrane, C. 'Fresh doubts on the Rufus Tradition'. *Hampshire Magazine*, February 1971.

Collins, F. S. *The language of god*. Free Press, 2006.

Cosgrove, D. 'The geometry of landscape'. In D. Cosgrove and S. Daniels (eds.) *The iconography of landscape*. CUP, 1988.

Cotterell, Arthur. *A dictionary of world mythology*. Book Club Associates, 1979.

De Santillana, Georgio, and von Dechend, Hertha. *Hamlet's mill: An essay investigating the origins of human knowledge and its transmission through myth*. David R Godine, Boston, 1969.

Dilke, O. A. W. *Mathematics and measurement*. British Museum, 1987.

Dilke, O. A. W. *The Roman land surveyors*. David and Charles, 1971.

Ekwall, Eilert. *English river names*. Clarendon Press, 1928.

Engles, D. W. *Alexander the Great and the logistics of the Macedonian army*. University Presses of California, Columbia, and Princeton, 1980.

Frazer, J. G. *The golden bough*. Macmillan, 1890.

Freeman, Edward A. *The history of the Norman Conquest in England*. Clarendon Press, 1876.

Frost, C. *Time, space and order: the making of medieval Salisbury*. Peter Lang, 2009.

Godwin, Joscelyn. *Mystery religions of the ancient world*. Thames and Hudson, 1981.

Graves, Robert. *The white goddess*. Faber and Faber, 1961.

Graves, Robert. *The Greek myths*. Penguin, 1960.

Green, Martin. *A landscape revealed: 10,000 years on a chalkland farm*. Tempus, 2000.

Habachi, Labib. *The obelisks of Egypt*. Dent, 1978.

Harte, Jeremy. *English holy wells: a sourcebook*. Heart of Albion Press, 2008.

Hartley, J. B. 'Maps, knowledge and power'. In D. Cosgrove and S. Daniels (eds.) *The iconography of landscape*. CUP, 1988.

Knight, C., and Lomas, R. *Uriel's machine*. Century, 1999.

Lemprier, J. *Bibliotheca classica*. London, 1825.

Lewis, C. T., and Short, C. *A Latin dictionary*. Clarendon Press, 1896.

Lomazzo, Giovanni. *Idea del tempio della pictura*. Milan, 1590.

Malory, Thomas. *Le morte d'Arthur*. William Caxton, 1485.

Maltwood, Kathleen E. *A guide to Glastonbury's temple of the stars*. London, 1929.

Marriot, C. A. *SkyMap version 2.2.8*. Computer program, 1995.

Matthew, H. C. G. and Harrison, B. (eds.) *Oxford Dictionary of National Biography*. OUP, 2004.

Meinig, D. W. 'Symbolic landscapes'. *The interpretation of ordinary landscapes*. OUP, 1979.

Mellersh, N. and J. *The ballad of Red Rufus*. Melersh, 2000.

Michell, John. *New light on the ancient mysteries of Glastonbury*. Gothic Image Publications, 1990.

Milner, J. In *Gentleman's Magazine*, 1789.

North, John. *Stonehenge: Neolithic man and the cosmos*. HarperCollins, 1996.

North, John. *The ambassadors' secret*. Orion, 2004.

Penny, A. and Wood, J. E. 'The Dorset Cursus complex'. *The Archaeological Journal*, 1973.

Pollock, John. *Harold Rex: Is King Harold II buried in Bosham Church?* Penny Royal, 1996.

Redondi, P. (trans. Raymond Rosenthal). *Galileo: heretic*. Princeton University Press, 1987.

Ross, Anne. *Pagan Celtic Britain*. Sphere Books, 1974.

Russell, Bertrand. *Autobiography*. Allen & Unwin, 1967-1969.

Rykwert, J. *The idea of a town: the anthropology of urban form in Rome, Italy and the ancient world*. Faber and Faber, 1976.

Sandars, N. K. (ed.) *The epic of Gilgamesh*. Penguin, 1972.

Schama, Simon. *Landscape and memory*. Fontana, 1996.

Schilling, Govert. 'Stars fell on Muggenburg'. *New Scientist*, 16 December 1995.

Sculley, Vincent. *The earth, the temple, and the gods: Greek sacred architecture*. Yale, 1979.

Smyth, Alfred. *King Alfred the Great*. OUP, 1995.

Sumner, Heywood. *The ancient earthworks of Cranbourne Chase*. Chiswick Press, 1913.

Sumner, Heywood. *The ancient earthworks of the New Forest*. Chiswick Press, 1917.

Taylor, John H. *Death and the afterlife in ancient Egypt*. British Museum Press, 2001.

Thom, Alexander. *Megalithic sites in Britain*. Clarendon Press, 1967.

Thom, Alexander. *Megalithic lunar observatories*. Clarendon Press, 1971.

White, Michael. *Galileo: antichrist*. Weidenfeld & Nicolson, 2007.

Wood, Michael. *In search of England*. Viking Press, 1999.

INDEX